Reader's Digest

READING skill BUILDER™

ADVANCED

PROJECT EDITOR: **WARREN J. HALLIBURTON**

EDITOR: **TERRY COOPER**

CONSULTANTS:

Jorge Garcia, Ed. D.
Supervisor Secondary Reading
Hillsborough County Public
Schools
Tampa, Florida

Susan Pasquini
Reading Specialist/
English Instructor
Escondido High School
San Diego, California

Frank Vernol
Instructional Learning
Secondary Reading
Dallas Independent School
District
Dallas, Texas

Grace Whittaker
Secondary Reading Supervisor
Boston Public Schools
Boston, Massachusetts

READER'S DIGEST EDUCATIONAL DIVISION
The credits and acknowledgments that appear on the inside
back cover are hereby made a part of this copyright page.
© 1980 by Reader's Digest Services, Inc., Pleasantville, N.Y. 10570. All rights reserved,
including the right to reproduce this book or parts thereof in any form.
Printed in the United States of America.

Reader's Digest ® Trademark Reg. U.S. Pat. Off. Marca Registrada ISBN 0-88300-282-4

□□□ □□□ □□□ Part 3   Reorder No. B34

SiLVER EdiTiON

CONTENTS

📼   Stories for which Audio Lessons are available.

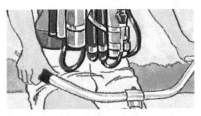

4

Record- Breaking Flight

Terry Cooper

The announcement that an American team was planning to cross the Atlantic in a balloon was greeted with the usual curiosity. The crew members were Ben Abruzzo, Max Anderson and Larry Newman, all from Albuquerque, New Mexico. They would launch their enormous silvery ship, the *Double Eagle II* (97 feet high and 65 feet across; 29.56 by 19.81 meters), from Presque Isle, Maine. Their destination: Paris, France, more than 3,000 miles (5,000 kilometers) away.

Public interest was tempered by the fact that, since the first attempt in 1873, 17 teams had tried this crossing, and each flight had failed. Among those who had failed were two members of the *Double Eagle II* crew. While many Americans as well as Europeans followed the news of the imminent launching, they knew that the odds were heavily on the side of the disappointing statistics.

The Double Eagle II crew members had good reason to hope that this time the flight would end differently. After all, they were highly trained airplane pilots who had committed thousands of hours to developing and perfecting the techniques they would need for the flight. Their equipment and provisions were meticulously packed in the 6½-by-6-foot (2.74-by-1.83-meter) gondola built to do double duty as a sea-worthy craft in case of an emergency ocean landing.

In addition to an ample supply of food (coffee, cocoa, doughnuts, raisins, sardines, olives, hot dogs, bagels, lox and vitamins) and water, other necessities were stowed in the gondola, including 600 pounds (272 kilograms) of lead and 5450 pounds (2472 kilograms) of sand, oxygen masks, computers to help in navigation, foul-weather gear, a portable heater, and a radio that would transmit signals to a Nimbus 6 satellite which would then relay the balloon's position to the Goddard Space Center in Washington, D.C.

But the weather remained the ultimate factor to be reckoned with in the flight. As explained by Bob Rice of Weather Services Corporation of New Bedford, Massachusetts, "Most of these flights fail because they deviate to the north or south. The biggest hazard is an Azores high, which can grab a balloon and drift it south between the Azores and Portugal; the craft would continue south and west and never recover. So you look for a pattern that is going to minimize the Azores influence and also protect you from any push to the north."

The aeronauts waited anxiously until meteorologists reported ideal weather for flying. Then, on Friday evening, August 11, 1978, at 5:35 p.m., they began final preparations, including inflating the balloon with helium. About three hours later, at 8:43 p.m., the crew clambered aboard, and *Double Eagle II* lifted off heading north, leaving Presque Isle far below.

The absence of ceremony in the launching suggested little of ballooning's rich history. Although mentioned as early as the 1200s, it was not until 1783 that two brothers, Jacques Etienne and Joseph Michel Montgolfier, actually designed and constructed a balloon that successfully transported living beings. Held aloft by air heated and expanded by burning charcoal in a pan beneath the bag, the vessel carried a duck, a rooster and a sheep. This flight, only eight minutes long, began an era of ballooning during which human passengers would ultimately be carried.

Around the time of the Montgolfier flight, J.A.C. Charles was working on a hydrogen balloon, safer and more buoyant than hot-air balloons. (Hydrogen is seven times lighter than air.) This balloon was similar in operation to balloons used today. Modern-day balloons (like *Double Eagle II*) are made of plastic or nylon and inflated with one of three gases—hydrogen, helium or coal gas. At the top of the bag is a valve, which the pilot controls from below by pulling a cord that releases gas in order to lower the balloon. The bottom of the bag ends in a tube called an appendix through which gas is fed into the balloon. Below the balloon is the passengers' gondola or basket attached to the bag by ropes; it is usually made of wicker, which is light in weight.

From the end of the 1700s, ballooning caught on quickly both as a vehicle for scientific study and as a sport. Adventurers began setting one record after another—for example, the first balloon to traverse the English Channel; the first parachutist to jump from a balloon; the first balloon to lift off in the United States. Inevitably ballooning became a sport with a worldwide following, reaching its greatest popularity in the early 1900s. Even after that time, zealous pilots never lost their thirst for seeing who could stay up the longest and travel the farthest.

The crew of the *Double Eagle II* was determined to achieve that distinction as they took to the air. After a slight disturbance just after liftoff, all proceeded smoothly for several days. One crew member de-

Adventurers make the first balloon crossing of the English Channel in 1785.

scribed what those peaceful days were like: "There are no books or music up there, but there is the whole world to see. It's completely silent, and you move with the clouds. When you come over land, you are standing on a balcony and the world going by underneath you is such a magnificent sight that you have to force yourself to sleep when it is time to do so."

Double Eagle II soars over the southern coast of England.

▲ Smiling crew members return greetings of well-wishers at landing site of their record-breaking flight.

By Monday traveling at 15,000 feet (4572 meters) and an average speed of 12 mph (19.3 kph), *Double Eagle II* skirted the northeast coast of Newfoundland. On Tuesday the balloon was within 1000 miles (1609 kilometers) of Ireland. Then the relatively quiescent voyage took a turn for the worse. The threat of a violent storm necessitated taking the balloon to 20,000 feet (6096 meters). This meant freezing temperatures, the fear of frostbite and the use of oxygen masks. Still it was a minor crisis compared with what would happen the next day.

Suddenly, on Wednesday afternoon *Double Eagle II* drifted into a cold mass that caused it to lose its ability to heat itself. The balloon dipped dangerously from 22,000 feet (6705 meters) to 4000 feet (1219 meters). In a panic the crew threw most of the ballast, the sleeping bags and nearly everything else out of the gondola. "We were scared stiff," recalled Anderson. Luckily, they drifted into a warm open spot in the clouds. The warm afternoon sun shining through saved the day. After several hours of warming, *Double Eagle II* ascended to a safer

Crew members line up to answer questions for a curious public.

altitude once again.

Sometime later the wind, a vital force in ballooning, died. Was this the end of the line? Would the balloon be forced to land in the sea? Would this expedition be added to the long list of unsuccessful ones? As the crew prepared for the inevitable, a fresh breeze picked up and swooped the balloon over Wales and across the English Channel.

As the *Double Eagle II* neared the French coast, it was spotted by a group of airplanes and helicopters that escorted it to its final destination—a sunlit wheatfield crowded with thousands of well-wishers, about 60 miles (96.5 kilometers) northwest of Paris.

Though somewhat short of their intended landing place at Le Bourget airport in Paris (where the Lone Eagle, Charles Lindbergh, had landed on the first transatlantic airplane flight some 51 years before), the crew was elated with their daring feat. At 7:49 p.m. they dumped the last of their ballast and began the descent. No sooner had they touched down than the crowd engulfed them, ripping off pieces of the once lofty balloon to keep as souvenirs of the historic event.

After an eventful six-day journey, Double Eagle II touches down in a field not far from Paris, France.

Abruzzo remembers the landing this way: "As we came down, the sun was shining and all around were fields, beautiful fields with thousands of people pouring into them. As soon as we touched ground, we were surrounded. I was pleased and satisfied to be on the ground but I was sad, too. We wanted to make Le Bourget, but the winds just weren't favorable. We were only 50 or so miles (80.45 kilometers) short. But we did cover over 3,000 miles (482 kilometers) in just under six days, we set the world distance record and we crossed the Atlantic. We can't complain."

Why did they go was a recurrent question asked of the *Double Eagle II* crew. Abruzzo answered, "Unless frontiers are challenged from time to time—whether they be flying a balloon, breaking an altitude record in a plane or writing a fine piece of literature—we don't move forward as a society."

Number of Words: 1415 ÷ _____ Minutes Reading Time = Rate _____

I. OUTLINING

Complete the outline below by copying the letter of each word or group of words in the proper place.

a. scientific study
b. coal gas
c. who could stay up the longest and travel the farthest
d. weather

   I.   There are three different types of balloons.
        A.   hydrogen
        B.   helium
        C.   _____

  II.   Balloons were used for two main purposes.
        A.   sport
        B.   _____

 III.   Adventurers set records in balloons.
        A.   the first balloon to fly across the English Channel
        B.   the first balloon to lift off in the U.S.
        C.   _____

  IV.   Two important factors contributed to the success of the *Double Eagle II* balloon flight.
        A.   skill
        B.   _____

10 points for each correct answer   SCORE: _____

II. FACT/OPINION

Put an F next to each statement of fact and an O next to each statement that expresses an opinion.

_____ **1.** Seventeen teams had tried to cross the Atlantic in balloons, and seventeen teams had failed.

_____ **2.** The world underneath you is such a magnificent sight that you have to force yourself to sleep.

_____ **3.** Hydrogen is seven times lighter than air.

_____ **4.** It was not until 1783 that two brothers designed and constructed a balloon that carried living beings.

_____ **5.** The crew members had reasons for their hopes that this time the flight would end differently.

_____ **6.** Unless frontiers are challenged, we will not move forward as a society.

5 points for each correct answer   SCORE: _____

III. MAIN IDEA

Put an M next to the three sentences that state main ideas about this story.

_____ **1.** The *Double Eagle II* flight was a dangerous adventure.

_____ **2.** The *Double Eagle II* flight was a historic event.

_____ **3.** The *Double Eagle II* carried sardines in its gondola.

_____ **4.** Gondolas are usually made of wicker.

_____ **5.** People are constantly challenging their environment in different ways.

10 points for each correct answer   SCORE: _____

PERFECT TOTAL SCORE: 100   TOTAL SCORE: _____

IV. QUESTION FOR THOUGHT

Ben Abruzzo believes that frontiers must be challenged from time to time in order that we may move forward as a society. What does he mean by this comment?

The Perfect Crime

Jean Shepherd

My father loved used cars even more than he loved the White Sox, if possible. A used-car nut is even more dedicated than the ordinary car worshiper. A true zealot never thinks in terms of a *new* model. His entire frame of reference and system of values is based on acquiring someone else's troubles. It is a dangerous game, and the uncertainty of it appeals to the true used-car *lover*.

My father, in company with other used-car fanatics, loved to spend long Saturday afternoons roaming the used-car lots on the South Side of Chicago, beating the bushes for great buys and spectacular deals. And when the used-car type actually tracked his car down and made the buy, it was a total commitment. All the way. And if the car turned out to be actually functional, his love for it far exceeded the love and involvement of the ordinary man who simply went to a dealer and bought a new car.

Anybody can buy a new car and expect to get a fairly operative machine, but it takes guts, knowledge and a reckless sense of abandon to come home with, say, a Lafayette Six previously owned by other shadowy drivers and to feel confident of victory. A used car, therefore, is a far more powerful love object than a new one. And my father played this game to the hilt. Each successive used car was loved and babied, petted and honored in its turn.

Some of the great emotional scenes of his life occurred on used-car lots when he was deserting the Pontiac Eight for the "new" DeSoto. He would even go back day after day to see if the Pontiac was treated well, and, when it finally disappeared forever off the lot, he would get moody and morose.

Cars at that time had distinctive personalities and characteristics and did not all come stamped out of the same mold, painted with the same paint and advertised by the same agency. I remember spending long afternoons with my father, hunting for a particular Graham-Paige that reputedly was one of the finest.

The day we found that beautiful midnight blue, four-door Graham, with its big rugged radiator grille, was one of the true festival days of that time. She sat between an elderly Plymouth and a bulky LaSalle, glowing darkly with a sort of prim, contained politeness—a true aristocrat unaccountably cast in among the rabble. She had more than a few years on her but was spotless and ageless.

The old man lit up like a Christmas tree and immediately went into his cagey used-car buyer's cool, calculating, bargaining character. It was exciting in several ways. The contest between Father and *his* Friendly Fred, the imminent loss of the trusty old Pontiac— did the Graham have a sponge-rubber transmission? The lurking reefs of disaster were always there.

Later, the first time he wheeled the midnight-blue Graham up the driveway and around the back was just the beginning of it—the weeklong Festival of Love for the new Graham.

At that time I was just below the legal minimum age for driving. And I used to sit in the back seat and watch my father shift gears, casually make left

turns, back into parking spots and wheel the Graham around like a second skin.

In the Midwest driving is like breathing. Kids living on the Maine coast learn to sail at a certain age. They all do. In the Midwest driving is simply part of life, and the folks there are serious about it. Afternoons, when the car was parked in back, I would sit in the front seat and practice shifting gears, working the clutch and mental-ly whistling down US 41 in the center lane. And once in a very great while, when we would go out for a drive on a Sunday, my father would let me back the car out of the driveway.

I was always trying to curry favor with both the Graham and my father by surprising him, especially on Sundays. The surprise consisted of washing the Graham or polish-ing the chrome with some pink stuff that my father used.

One Sunday I was in the garage steadfastly working on the front bumper. The family was going out that night, and I was about to surprise everybody with a spectacular job on the chrome. I polished the rims on the headlights, and it's a tough and self-abusive job. My knuckles were scraped and my fingernails torn, the pink stuff soaking into my skin, but the grille was beautiful, just beautiful. And then I decided to back the car out of the garage by myself to really surprise them so that when they came out on the back porch they would see this blinding vision of flashing chrome.

I could imagine them saying: "Why, what has happened to the Graham-Paige? It looks better than new!"

And I would just stand proudly, modestly by and wait for the praise and the honor that would be due me.

I finally finished the job. The Graham was glistening. I scrunched down in the driver's seat and started the engine. What a sense of power! I checked the ammeter; it was flickering slightly on the "charge" side. Gas gauge— quarter full. Oil pressure—40 pounds (18 kilograms). Normal. The car hummed reassuringly.

I eased the clutch in and gently moved the gearshift lever into Reverse. Already I was a master of gearshifting. "Ease out on the clutch gently," I told myself and I began to roll backward out of the garage.

Screeeeeeeaaaa. . . .

I slammed on the brake and the clutch and hung in midair for a split second.

Egad! I had scraped the left rear fender on the garage door! I put her in First and tried to roll forward.

Eeeeaawwwrrrrr.

It was stuck! The fender was dragging against the door. I was sweating. And sick with fear. I had *really* done it this time, all the way!

I quickly scrunched over to the other side of the seat and got out. I was going to push the car into the garage. I couldn't move it. It was really stuck! I had to drive it in again.

I got behind the wheel and put it into First. I was going to do it real slowly. Real slow. . . .

EEEEEEEEAAARRRHHHH. BOING!

I could hear the door crunching and ripping. I got out again and looked. I could just see the edge of a huge scrape mark on that beautiful, midnight-blue fender. The paint was peeling off in long curls. It was

jammed, and I didn't know what to do. I knew that if I moved any further I'd strip off more paint. I had to do it!

I eased out on the clutch.

RRRRRRRR

It was stuck!

I could hear people moving in the house, doors slamming. Any minute now somebody was going to come out! I just knew it. My father! He was going to come out in the backyard to look in the trunk or to pick up a football or something.

The screen door flew open, and it was my kid brother. I headed him off.

"Hey Ran, hey. Would you go down in the basement? See if you can find my old ... ah ... my ... remember that old skyrocket I had? See if you can find my old skyrocket, will you, Ran? Go on, Ran, see if you can find it for me."

He looked at me and then went back in the house and down in the basement.

I didn't want anyone to know what I had done, and time was running out!

I leaped in the car. Any minute now my Old Man was going to come out. I knew it. I slammed it in gear.

EEEEEeeeuuunk!

It was free!

I turned the key off and got out. There it was! The back fender neatly peeled, a long scratch along the fender. What was I going to do?

I knew what to do. Nothing! Absolutely nothing!

Five minutes later I was two blocks away, knocking out fly balls and pretending I had never seen a car in my life.

That night we were all dressed up and in the Graham. I was in the back seat and worried sick. Nobody had even noticed that the back fender was scraped. I was keeping my mouth shut, and I was sweating, sizzling with guilt, fighting against the urge to blurt out:

"Stop the car! Look at the left rear fender! I did it! I am guilty! I am unworthy to exist in the nest of such a wonderful, innocent group. I am guilty and despicable!! Rotten to the core!!"

But what did I do? The same thing that modern man always does. Plays it cool. At least as cool as it is possible to be while shuddering under wave after wave of fear, guilt and remorse.

My father parked the car, and we went into the movie. I was still relatively safe. Darkness had obscured the raw wounds of my crime.

I squirmed through the movie in a cold sweat, barely able to keep the appearance of concentrating on my taffy apple.

Another crucial moment came when we approached the Graham in the parking lot. I hung back, anticipating the thunderclap.

It did not come. The Chief merely got in the front seat and said:

"Pile in. Let's go."

I scrunched down in the back seat and in my relief and nervousness talked a blue streak all the way home.

But later, in bed, the old icy sweat came back. He would *have* to see it tomorrow, and he would know! There was no escape! I squirmed and sweated for half an hour or so, and then developed a gigantic gut-heaving stomachache. My mother dragged me into the john, limp and wan, and hung my head over the bowl.

"That'll teach you to listen to me about all that junk you always eat."

For even in my pain, I had decided. "Is Dad awake?" I groaned, and without awaiting her answer, marched to the master's room to confess my perfect crime.

Number of Words: 1678 ÷ _____ Minutes Reading Time = Rate _____

I. SEQUENCE

Number the following statements from 1 to 5, according to the order in which they appear in the selection.

_____ **a.**   I decided to back the car out of the garage myself.

_____ **b.**   I developed a gigantic gut-heaving stomachache.

_____ **c.**   I had scraped the left rear fender on the garage door.

_____ **d.**   I could hear my mother shouting for me through the kitchen door so I dragged myself home.

_____ **e.**   I was two blocks away, knocking out fly balls.

5 points for each correct answer   SCORE: _____

II. PROBLEM SOLVING

Circle the letter (a, b or c) that tells how the characters in the story dealt with the following problems.

1.   The author scraped the car fender.
     a.   He reported the incident to his father right away.
     b.   He slipped away quietly, ignoring the situation.
     c.   He had the car fixed as soon as it happened.

2.   The author's father loved used cars.
     a.   He never bought one because he never found a good enough deal.
     b.   He had ten at all times.
     c.   He spent Saturday afternoons roaming the used car lots.

3.   The author's kid brother came out to the garage.
     a.   The author screamed at him.
     b.   The author told him the truth.
     c.   The author asked him to go down to the basement to find an old toy.

5 points for each correct answer   SCORE: _____

III. STORY ELEMENTS

Circle the letter (a, b or c) that correctly completes each sentence.

1. "The Perfect Crime" is
    a. ironic.   **b.** bizarre.   **c.** humorous.

2. The climax of this story occurs when
    a. the author scrapes the fender of his father's car.
    b. the author's father discovers the damage to the car.
    c. the parking-lot owner decides to pay to fix the car.

3. This story is told in the

    a. first person.   **b.** third person.   **c.** present tense.

---

10 points for each correct answer   SCORE: _____

IV. LANGUAGE USAGE

Use the following verbs to fill in the blanks: scrunched, squirmed, ease.

1. I quickly _____ over to the other side of the seat.

2. I _____ through the movie in a cold sweat.

3. When my father let me drive I'd _____ the clutch out.

---

10 points for each correct answer   SCORE: _____

PERFECT TOTAL SCORE: 100   TOTAL SCORE: _____

V. QUESTIONS FOR THOUGHT

Do you think the author did the right thing by not admitting what he had done to his father? Do you think the fear of an unpleasant reception or consequence should be a deterrent to admitting guilt?

The Best of Worlds

Douglas S. Looney

Laboring on one side of the net, U.S. Senator Lowell Weicker (R., Conn.) mutters, "Come on, Senator, what kind of shot is that?" On a court nearby, Senator Howard Metzenbaum (D., Ohio) misses shots at a record pace and complains after each one, "Oh, you dummy!"

But things brighten for Weicker when he hits a strong forehand that sends the opposition, Donna Dearborn and her partner, running into each other. Weicker's mood shifts from despair to deviousness. "Hey, Donna," Weicker says, "I was hoping you'd knock each other cold. Then I would cite the rule calling for continuous play and declare myself the winner." Senators are sharp on rules, especially when they're losing. Dearborn smiles, winningly.

She always smiles winningly. For good reason. What does she have to frown about? By age 24, Donna Dearborn was a tennis pro at John Gardiner's Tennis Ranch in Arizona's Paradise Valley, near Phoenix. Paradise Valley is sun-blessed and one of the nation's ranking splendors. "When I tell my friends I teach tennis here," Dearborn says, "they say, 'That's nice, but what's your *real* job?' "

That is her real job. She stands in the sun and recommends, "Bend your knees." Meanwhile, she is deepening her tan, which causes an elderly lady from Pittsburgh to look at her and say, "When I grow up, I want to look just like her." Dearborn teaches tennis to and often plays tennis with celebrities, like Ken Rosewall, who hangs out at Gardiner's between tournaments. She has played with Merv Griffin and, more recently, with John Scali, former United Nations ambassador.

Life at Gardiner's does not have many sharp edges for Donna Dearborn of Brattleboro, Vermont.

"This is a gentle job for Donna," says her boss, John Gardiner. "She's with people when they're nice." And there is no heavy lifting. One of her colleagues, 20-year-old Paul Gallery of West Covina, California, says, "This is ridiculous, to get paid for teaching a game in a place like this."

So what do you say about a woman who is young, beautiful, single and talented? About a woman who plays tennis with the stars by day and studies the stars above by night? About a woman with a college degree in mathematics who is

Dearborn often fills out in double games with people from all walks of life, including U.S. senators, TV stars and other tennis pros.

involved with a game she loves and can play as much as she wants? Dearborn says, "I can't imagine ever being any happier than I am now."

It is unlikely that the millions who awake hating every weekday morning can fathom the life of Donna Dearborn. "Sometimes," she says, "this job isn't as glamorous as my friends think, but I kind of like the fact they think it is. Besides, if I told them it wasn't glamorous, they wouldn't believe me, anyway." Her friends would be right.

"I am doing something I believe in," she says. "At the end of the day I feel like I've done something important. I've helped others have fun and I've had fun." Her joy at work flows from the clients—and some-

Some of the sun-blessed splendor of Paradise Valley

times from their excuses. One student says, "Donna, I can't play as well here because the sun is so much brighter than it is at home." Another says, "I can't hit high balls because the people I play with back home all hit low ones."

How did Dearborn fall into this lap of luxury and contentment? Blind, stupid luck is the most plausible explanation. Being a tennis pro was not a dream she had as a youngster. She got into sports playing tackle football with boys and went on through a progression of sports, most notably field hockey. A tennis racket didn't touch her hand until she was in high school. "I tried it," she says, "and something good happened. The ball went over the net." Her father, Frank, is superintendent of Brattleboro's Recreation and Parks Department, and she learned from his strokes, "which weren't wonderful."

For most of her growing-up years, her main squeeze was math. She'd ride her red Schwinn bicycle down by Pleasant Valley Reservoir where she would sit and work out geometry proofs until her heart was content. At Springfield College in Massachusetts, she continued to play tennis. But more important, she met Bruce Wright, then a faculty member and now a doctor for sick tennis strokes, who was heavily into tennis and who conveyed the sport's excitement to Dearborn. "With Donna," he says, "the racket is her brush and the court is her canvas." Donna went to North Carolina State for graduate work in applied math. "But when I got there," she says, "it seemed to me that being 22 years old and spending 20 hours a day with math books wasn't right." She decided to leave school and play in tennis tournaments, which she did, driving around in an old jalopy that consumed more oil than gas.

Her job enables Dearborn to combine her skills as a tennis player and a teacher.

She was determined to follow tennis to California or Florida. A friend offered a ride to Phoenix in the summer of 1976, and once in the Valley of the Sun, Dearborn found a "house with no windows propped up on cinder blocks with a mangy horse in the back." She had just spread her sleeping bag on the floor when the black widow and tarantula exterminator showed up.

After plenty of job-looking, she eventually went to Gardiner's, her toes protruding through raggedy sneakers and

Dearborn, during one of her early-morning workouts

with no racket to demonstrate her talents. Head pro Bill Foulk said, "You've got to wear whites all the time, maybe clean bathrooms and always smile." Said Donna Dearborn, "It sounds like the Army here and you're the general." A few days later she was hired. Foulk says, "She could play the game well, she was attractive and personable and had a college degree and teaching experience. I'd take a hundred like her."

By 6:45 a.m. daily, Donna is out running—a 12-mile jaunt around the desert as the cottontails dart about the cactus plants and mesquite and the sun begins poking pink behind the Superstition Mountains. (In December she ran Arizona's Fiesta Bowl Marathon in 3:18:15 to qualify for the Boston Marathon.) "I love the sunrise," she says while jogging easily. "Especially these days when the sun is rising and the moon is setting at the same time. Plus I feel better because I've accomplished something before the day has even started for most people." Then it's 50 sit-ups, 25 push-ups and a breakfast consisting of "an apple and orange going into the shower."

Most of the rest of the day is spent teaching tennis. Or

stringing rackets in the pro shop. Or sometimes working as a court keeper, which means keeping things all spruced up because, as pro Jeff Stewart says, "Nobody learns from an unmade bed." Sometimes Dearborn is a hostess, meaning that for $12 an hour she plays tennis with a client, most often to fill out a doubles game. Sometimes she gives private lessons.

Things do go wrong in Camelot: Dearborn sprained an ankle stepping on a tennis ball; picking up some wooden blocks used in instruction, she got splinters in her hand, then went out and played terribly in a doubles match in which she was partnered with Rosewall. "He's only my favorite player," she sighs, "and I've only looked at one of his instructional films about 80 times." And she muses about the sameness in the weather and her life: "I suppose I could use more variety," she says. True, a day filled with nothing but backhands can glaze a person's eyes.

But she does lead the good life, and she knows it. Sometimes it's the Phoenix Symphony; sometimes it's astronomy

classes at Scottsdale Community College; sometimes a course in cabinetmaking. She goes to Montana during the winter to cross-country ski. One summer when the weather in Arizona was stifling, she taught at another Gardiner facility in Sun Valley, Idaho.

One night, after nearly 12 hours in the sun, Donna Dearborn returned to her apartment, put Brahms' Piano Concerto No. 2 on the stereo, and dropped into a vinyl chair, too tired to even face fixing her newest favorite food—broiled bananas with honey on top. Yet even the exhaustion is part of the good life. As Bruce Wright says, "What makes for an enviable job? That you hardly work? Nonsense." But will Dearborn forevermore stand against this lovely backdrop coaxing cheerily, "Watch the ball?"

"Sometime," she says, "maybe I'll go where there are really big mountains, a good university and tennis courts. But just being here and teaching people a game that can bring them so much pleasure, it's hard to imagine anything any better than this."

Number of Words: 1442 ÷ _____ Minutes Reading Time = Rate _____

I. SUPPORTING DETAILS

Match the people (column A) listed below with the careers (column B) each has pursued. Write the letter (a, b, c, d or e) for each profession on the appropriate line.

	A		B
_____ **1.**	Ken Rosewall	**a.**	U.S. senator
_____ **2.**	John Scali	**b.**	U.N. ambassador
_____ **3.**	Lowell Weicker	**c.**	T.V. host
_____ **4.**	John Gardiner	**d.**	tennis ranch owner
_____ **5.**	Merv Griffin	**e.**	tennis pro

5 points for each correct answer   SCORE: _____

II. CHARACTERIZATION

Check √ the four statements below that describe Donna Dearborn's character, as presented in the story.

_____ **1.**   She has a sunny personality, smiling often and making other people feel at ease.

_____ **2.**   She enjoys helping people, especially helping them to have fun on a tennis court.

_____ **3.**   She is very ambitious, and even as a girl wanted to become a top tennis player.

_____ **4.**   She likes to keep herself in good physical condition.

_____ **5.**   She is bored with her job, and wants to teach math.

_____ **6.**   She is realistic, and appreciates the good fortune she has had in life.

5 points for each correct answer   SCORE: _____

III. SEQUENCE

Number the events listed below in the order in which they occurred in Donna Dearborn's life.

_____ **a.** She found a job as a tennis pro in Arizona.

_____ **b.** She went to graduate school in mathematics.

_____ **c.** She played field hockey while in school.

_____ **d.** She followed tennis tournaments in an old car.

_____ **e.** She was offered a ride to Phoenix by a friend.

5 points for each correct answer   SCORE: _____

IV. LANGUAGE USAGE

The author uses descriptive language to make some of his points. Write the letter (a, b or c) for the sentence that matches the meaning of each sentence below.

a. It is a very beautiful place.
b. She looked a mess.
c. When playing tennis, she is an artist.

_____ **1.** Paradise Valley is one of the nation's ranking splendors.

_____ **2.** "The racket is her brush and the court is her canvas."

_____ **3.** Her toes protruded through raggedy sneakers.

10 points for each correct answer   SCORE: _____

PERFECT TOTAL SCORE: 100   TOTAL SCORE: _____

V. QUESTION FOR THOUGHT

Would you like to have the kind of life Donna Dearborn leads in Arizona? Take one side of this question and give your reasons.

An Incredible

Pointing to the large wall map in the Mount Isa police station in Queensland, Australia, Jessie Brown showed Inspector Jack Vaudin exactly where her 29-year-old son, Dennis, was stranded: on the Camooweal-Burketown road, about 100 miles (160 kilometers) south of the Gulf of Carpentaria. She described how she had chartered a light plane with her daughter-in-law and spotted her missing son bogged down in his truck, completely cut off by flood waters for miles in every direction.

"That's where he is," she said with anxious certainty. "And the water's coming up fast all around him."

"Don't worry," Vaudin promised. "We'll get him back."

Dennis Brown's troubles had begun four days earlier, on February 15, 1976, when he set out from his small cattle property, Frenchman's Gardens, bound for Mount Isa, a rough, tough, copper-mining city 155 miles (249 kilometers) to the south. He was trying to make the journey before a gathering tropical storm struck the area. In the wet season between Christmas and the end of March, up to 18 inches (46 centimeters) of rain have been known to fall in 24 hours in this area. Flooding often maroons remote Outback communities.

Trek
Timothy Hall

Brown had been driving for seven consecutive hours when suddenly his four-wheel-drive truck gave a sickening lurch, and its front wheels plunged through the surface of the road. He climbed out and immediately sank to his waist in bubbling, sulfur-smelling mud that sucked at his legs like quicksand. He had driven straight into one of the most deceptive and treacherous traps awaiting the unwary driver in the Outback. A hardrock base 15 feet (4 meters) below the road prevents the water that runs off the hills from seeping away. Gradually the subsoil becomes saturated, but the sun-baked surface forms a hard crust.

This crust is strong enough to support a man, even a horse, but any vehicle that ventures onto it becomes hopelessly trapped.

Brown knew that he would never make it out on foot. His left leg had been crippled by childhood polio, and he walked with a pronounced limp. The nearest settlement, Gregory Downs (population 12), was some 40 miles (64 kilometers) away. And, because the monsoon season had begun, the chance was remote that another vehicle would come along.

That night 4 inches (10 centimeters) of rain fell in less than an hour. All the next day Brown

struggled to dig out the truck, but when darkness fell it was even deeper into the mire. He had no choice but to wait for rescue.

By Wednesday he was down to his last tin of meat. The temperature climbed to above 100° Fahrenheit (38° Centigrade), and the heat and humidity sapped his strength.

On Thursday morning the search plane appeared overhead and dropped food. He waved frantically to show that he was alive and well, and for the moment his growing despair was lifted.

From Mount Isa headquarters, Inspector Vaudin had in-structed two of his most competent policemen—Sergeant Ray Brank, 39, and Constable Graham Robson, 23—to "do anything necessary" to rescue Dennis Brown. Brand and Robson packed emergency supplies into a four-wheel-drive police truck and quickly set out from Camooweal, 100 miles (160 kilometers) southeast of the stranded Brown.

As they headed north, the road became increasingly treacherous. They bounced in and out of potholes, crept through sand and flooded creeks, slid almost out of control in black mud. For hundreds of yards at a stretch, the road disappeared under water. Not until 9:15 p.m., six hours out of Camooweal, did they finally sight Dennis Brown. "I thought I'd seen every emotion until I saw the sheer relief and happiness on Brown's face," Brand recalled later.

But this joy soon turned to despair: as the police truck took the strain on a towrope hooked to Brown's truck, more of the road surface collapsed. The rescue vehicle, too, became hopelessly mired. As hard as Brand and Robson worked, they, like Brown before them, succeeded only in forcing their vehicle still deeper into the bog. To make matters worse, their two-way radio proved useless amid the encircling hills.

Around 1 a.m., Robson proposed that he, as the fittest of the group and as a native Outbacker, should try to walk the 40 miles (64 kilometers) to Gregory Downs for assistance. At any other time it would have been an almost suicidal suggestion, but this was not a normal situation. Reluctantly, Sergeant Brand agreed. With no illusions about his chances of getting through in the heat of the day Robson set out alone into the night.

For the first 6 miles (10 kilometers), Robson made good progress through the grass

fields and spindly gum trees. Then his ears caught the sound of wildly rushing water. Out in the blackness he could hear branches and uprooted tree trunks crashing past in a creek that had become a torrent.

Robson took one step into the swirling current, then recoiled as he heard the deep-throated roar of a crocodile. All his life he had feared crocodiles, and he knew that the Gregory River, into which the creek emptied a few miles away, was a home for the man-eating brutes. Only weeks before, he had read about a hunter who had been devoured by a 20-foot (6-meter) crocodile.

For 10 minutes Robson stood rooted to the spot, straining for a clue to the crocodile's position. Then suddenly he remembered the urgency of his mission and felt ashamed. He had promised to get help, and here he was, too scared to go on.

Taking a deep breath, Robson walked boldly into the water and at chest depth dived in and was carried swiftly downstream—toward the crocodile. Branches crushed against him. As he reached up to push one away he felt something alive. To his horror he realized it was a snake—a big water python, frightened and twisting to de-

fend itself. Robson shuddered as the current carried the snake away, scraping its cold 6-foot (2-meter) length along his face. When he could finally touch bottom, he scrambled wildly up the bank, gasping for breath. His ordeal had scarcely begun, and already he had been exposed to his two greatest fears in the Outback—crocodiles and snakes.

For the next 10 miles (16 kilometers), Robson was in waist-deep water most of the time. He took off his sneakers, useless in the mud, and when his wet shorts started to chafe his skin he removed them as well. He slipped and fell repeatedly, bruising and cutting himself on the sharp rocks. Clouds of mosquitoes tormented him; leeches attached themselves to his ankles and feet, getting between his toes where he couldn't pull them off without stopping. When he did stop, enormous centipedes crawled up his legs and over his body. Their bite is painful, and bushmen swear that the pain returns every 12 months for the rest of a victim's life.

Yet Robson's greatest fear was still snakes, because he knew that, like him, venomous mulga and Australian brown snakes would be making for

the few remaining patches of high, dry ground. The thought of treading on one of those aggressive creatures haunted him through the night.

Three times the ground suddenly collapsed beneath him, and he thrashed about in water up to his neck, oozing mud sucking at his legs. Each time he was able to grab tufts of grass and laboriously drag himself out. Dripping, shaking and scared, he kept telling himself: "I must go on. I *must* get help!" In all his life in the bush he had never felt so alone, so vulnerable.

It began to rain as Robson plowed through the thick, black mud that separated the tufts of waist-high grass. The rain became a deluge. Far ahead Robson could see great forks of jagged lightning splitting the sky, a reminder of more storms and the ever-mounting danger to Dennis Brown and Sergeant Brand.

While Robson was thinking of their peril, he stepped on a big wild pig that leaped to its feet and snorted savagely. Robson ran to escape its charge and floundered through the mud.

The wet plain at night is never silent as millions of frogs, crickets and bugs croak, scrape and hum constantly.

The endless night finally

gave way to a dawn that probably saved Robson's life. Not 18 feet (5.5 meters) away, in the middle of his path, was one of the largest Australian brown snakes he had ever seen. Six feet (1.8 meters) long and as thick as his wrist, the deadly creature had already lifted its head to strike. For what seemed an eternity they stared at each other, and then very slowly and methodically Robson inched backward, his eyes never leaving the snake. Out of range of a strike, he bolted and ran.

As the temperature rose past 80° Fahrenheit (26° Centigrade) and the humidity climbed, Robson worried that he might be going mad and walking in circles—a very real danger in terrain without landmarks. His watch told him that time had passed, and he knew he must have walked a certain distance, but his senses told him that he was always in the same place.

He became obsessed with counting his footsteps. The carrion-eating black kites and piebald crows that hovered overhead grew threatening in his confused mind.

Plodding mechanically along, intent on staying on his feet, he was at first unaware of the rumbling sound ahead of him. When he finally did hear it, he could not quite comprehend what it was. When he shaded his eyes and realized the sound was made by a road grader, he sank to his knees at the edge of the muddy track, burying his head in his hands in exhaustion and relief.

The driver, Bill Bailey, noticed that Robson was badly sunburned, that blood was pouring from the chafed wounds on his legs and that his body was a mass of insect bites. He couldn't believe that in nine hours Robson had walked, scrambled and swum 40 miles (64 kilometers) over such arduous terrain. As for Robson, he touched the grader to make sure he wasn't imagining it and simultaneously repeated, over and over, that he must get to Brown and Brand.

Bailey took Robson into Gregory Downs, where they quickly assembled a rescue team. By 4:30 that afternoon, Friday, February 20, Robson was back where he had started his epic journey, having led a small convoy through the floods. A grateful Brown and Sergeant Brand were little the worse for their experience.

Back in Camooweal that evening—after 42 hours of continuous duty—Robson muttered

something to Brand about being "a bit weary," collapsed on a bed and slept for more than 12 hours.

Within days, messages of congratulation began arriving at police headquarters. The Queensland Police Department later gave Robson its highest award for bravery and devotion to duty, and the Royal Humane Society of Australasia presented him its silver medal for gallantry. And in February 1977, a year after his incredible journey, Robson was awarded the Stanhope Gold Medal, the British Humane Society's highest award, for the bravest act performed during the previous year throughout the entire British Commonwealth.

Dennis Brown takes great pleasure in the honors that have been bestowed on the young constable. He explains, "To endure those hardships for a person one has never seen before is surely the mark of a truly brave man."

Number of Words: 1921 ÷ _____ Minutes Reading Time = Rate _____

I. SEQUENCE

Number the following sentences in the order they appear in the story.

_____ **a.** Robson walked boldly into the water and was carried swiftly downstream—toward the crocodile.

_____ **b.** Robson set out alone in search of the nearest town.

_____ **c.** Robson inched backward very slowly, and when he was finally out of the snake's range, he ran.

_____ **d.** For the next 10 miles (16 kilometers) Robson was haunted by mosquitoes and leeches.

_____ **e.** Robson ran to escape the big wild pig's charge.

_____ **f.** By 4:30 Friday afternoon, Robson was back where he started his epic journey.

5 points for each correct answer   SCORE: _____

II. SUPPORTING DETAILS

Write a check ✓ next to the three sentences that support the idea that the Outback was a hazardous and difficult place in which to survive.

_____ **1.** In the middle of his path was one of the largest deadly Australian brown snakes he had ever seen.

_____ **2.** Three times the ground collapsed beneath him.

_____ **3.** Volcanic eruptions were commonplace.

_____ **4.** The wet plain at night is never silent.

_____ **5.** The temperature rose past 100° F. (38 C.).

10 points for each correct answer   SCORE: _____

III. CAUSE/EFFECT

Each set of statements has a cause and an effect. Write a C next to each cause and an E next to each effect.

_____ **1.** Dennis Brown was trapped in sulfur-smelling mud.

_____   Inspector Vaudin instructed two competent policemen to journey to the Outback.

_____ **2.** Constable Robson set out alone to seek help.

_____   The rescue vehicle, too, became hopelessly trapped.

_____ **3.** The land was bereft of landmarks.

_____   Robson worried that he was going mad and walking in circles.

10 points for each correct answer   SCORE: _____

IV. GENERALIZATIONS

Write a check ✓ next to two generalizations that could be made about Graham Robson.

_____ **1.** He was a man of his word.

_____ **2.** He loved the challenge of the flooded Outback.

_____ **3.** He displayed great endurance and courage.

5 points for each correct answer   SCORE: _____

PERFECT TOTAL SCORE: 100   TOTAL SCORE: _____

V. QUESTIONS FOR THOUGHT

Why did Graham Robson believe he had to go on? Why do you think a person's mental attitude affects his/her ability to survive?

Woody Allen Wipes the

Frank Rich

When Woody Allen, a hunched, frail figure in an army-green trench coat, walks the streets of New York, strangers don't treat him in quite the same way they do other show-business celebrities. They don't just gawk at him or shyly ask for his autograph. They yell out his first name as though he were an old pal and often follow him for blocks, trying to engage him in conversation. Allen's fans behave this way because they assume that the Woody Allen they see on the street is the same Woody Allen they've been seeing on their movie screens for many years. And why shouldn't they?

Ever since people began to pay attention to him, back when he was a stand-up comic in the early 1960s, Woody Allen has been making people laugh by playing a single character who is so affable, so human and so chummy that his fans feel they have an intimate, personal relationship with him. They couldn't be more wrong.

The Woody Allen who darts through the New York streets is not the easygoing, approachable person we think he is. When strangers try to detain him for more than a quick hello, the real Woody Allen turns pale, shrinks into his long coat like a turtle backing into its shell and walks away as fast as his short legs can carry him. Not for a second does he smile.

The real Woody Allen doesn't smile because he's serious—as serious a person as you might ever meet. Serious in the sense that he's never "on" when he isn't working. Serious in the sense that he tries hard to shield himself from all the social and business dealings that come with a highly successful show-biz career. Serious in the sense that he tries to live the ascetic life of an artist rather

Smile off His Face

than the public life of an entertainer. Serious in the sense that as an artist he's eager to confront some of the most important philosophical issues known to modern man. "Feelings of alienation, loneliness, emptiness—those areas are all my entertainment meat," Allen says, and he isn't joking.

Just how serious Woody Allen really is became clear to his public after the movie *Annie Hall* was released in 1977. Much of *Annie Hall* is funny in the usual Allen style, but parts of it aren't meant to be funny in the slightest; there's also a bittersweet ending. "Life is divided into the horrible and the miserable," Allen announces early in the movie, and he then goes on to support his case.

Shortly after seeing the film, I met Allen for lunch. He arrived wearing a plaid shirt, corduroy pants, an Ivy League tweed jacket and nondescript work shoes. After refusing a drink (he never drinks or smokes), he ordered up a couple of fried eggs. He talked freely, explaining that *Annie Hall* was indeed meant to be a departure from his previous movies, but added that it wasn't nearly as serious as the script he was working on.

"It's a personal view, but I have a lesser opinion of comedy. It's much harder to do than serious filmmaking—it's really hard to make an audience laugh and keep them laughing—but if it's tough, so what? A comedy, for me, has the quality of being a little des-

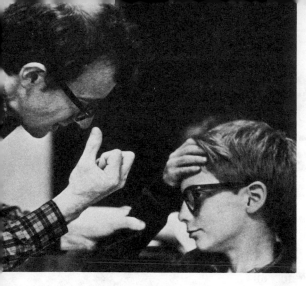

sert, a diversion. It's fun to see a Buster Keaton or a Chaplin film—and, of course, I have an irresistible enjoyment of the Marx Brothers; but to me it's all second features. The real meat and potatoes are serious films."

When it comes to describing what his serious movies would be like, Allen doesn't fool around. "Serious serious, dead serious," he said. "Not middle serious, but very heavy stuff, really heavy." He paused and looked around the room. "The type of drama that interests me most is personal drama, though there may not be a market for it. The drama I like is, for example, what you see in foreign films."

Allen's dead serious attitude also applies to his preoccupation with death. Aside from seeing a psychologist for twen-

ty years, Allen's only real way of coping with questions of death is through his work. He doesn't look at art as a solution to the dread of death, but making movies is at least a distraction, a way of avoiding "grimmer thoughts." He's grateful to spend a year making a film, during which he can be inundated with "small obstacles like casting and money and all that" and can enjoy "the catharsis of expressing inner feelings."

"I never get so depressed that it interferes with my work," he says. "I'm disciplined. I can go into a room every morning and churn it out." What most people don't realize about Woody Allen is that he has always been this way. He has been traumatized by the fear of death since he "first put a thought togeth-

A birthday scene from Woody Allen's 1978 film, *Interiors*.

er," and he has spent a lifetime in rooms churning out work, always setting up new challenges for himself.

He grew up in Flatbush, New York, in an ethnically mixed, "lower middle class, high poor" neighborhood. He devoted his days to playing ball (he is, contrary to popular belief, a good athlete), going to movies, watching wrestling on TV and reading Mickey Spillane novels and comic books. Even then he was a loner. "I never ever ate with the family," he says. "And I never ever did any extracurricular activities at school. I would go in at nine and come back at three. Then I'd go right into my bedroom and shut the door—immediately. Consequently, I was able to get some things done. I could learn an instrument. I became

really adept at sleight-of-hand tricks, which took me endless hours and which I can still do. My mother used to pass by the room and hear the coins dropping for eight hours."

He squeaked through Midwood High School with a 71 average, only to be kicked out of New York University in his freshman year. But outside of the educational system, he drove himself. His show-business career began when he started working long hours to perfect one-line gags that he could sell. This led to a $25-a-week gag-writing job and finally to highly paid writing assignments for all the major TV comedies of the 1950s. At the same time, he became a reader—forcing himself to read books "from the superstars like Shakespeare and Hemingway."

Given his compulsive shyness, it's hard to imagine how Allen ever became a performer. The turning point came when he saw Mort Sahl, a popular stand-up comic of the 1960s, perform. Woody was dazzled by Sahl, who was "high art and showed you could do serious work as a comic." Allen started working up his own act. Once he'd started, he wouldn't let go. For six months, he worked every night—for no pay—at a tiny and forlorn little joint called the Duplex in New York City's Greenwich Village. The "stage" was at the same level as the audience, which on some nights numbered only two or three customers. Though he was fired from his writing job on The Garry Moore Show and though he woke up each morning with a "nightmarish dread" of going on, Woody kept at it. The dread was never entirely conquered—but the rest, as they say, is history. A history that meant acclaim and a life in the public eye that Woody dislikes intensely and avoids as much as possible. The young Woody who went right home from school and shut himself in a room has grown into a man who practices the same habits. Allen wakes up early each morning to write, and he often writes at night, too. He devotes at least an hour a day to practicing his clarinet, often to the accompaniment of records. Even when he's shooting a film, he always shows up to play with his Dixieland jazz band at a club on Monday nights. At most, Allen will devote a half-hour a day to sheer idleness—"sitting around reading magazines."

Though he's much in demand, Allen doesn't go to many openings or parties. He won't go to an event where there are likely to be photographers or reporters, and when he does go to a party he'll often stand in a corner looking as if he's on his way out. Only basketball games, dinners with friends and new movies regularly draw him out into the real world.

But even when he does go out, Allen is very careful to avoid situations that make him anxious. He used to wear a khaki fishing hat for disguise, but the hat became a trademark around town and he abandoned it. He still hides within a hooded parka.

"I always had difficulty with people on a social level. Before, when I was shy and unknown, I thought that, if I could only

Allen practices the clarinet daily and plays in a Dixieland band once a week.

make it in some way, it would really help relieve me socially and I could relax and go to parties and do things. But then, as soon as I did become known, that became the problem. I thought, 'I'm well known—I can't go out.' There are times when I feel like—though it isn't true—but I feel like a prisoner in my own home; when I feel like, oh, I don't want to go down and get the papers because some people will say hello to me. So I stay in. My idea of a good time is to take a walk from my house to the office and not for the entire walk have to worry about hearing my name being called from a passing car or being spoken to at all. That would be perfect."

Number of Words: 1645 ÷ _____ Minutes Reading Time = Rate _____

I. VOCABULARY

Fill in each blank with the letter (a, b, c, d or e) of the correct word: a. affable, b. indictable, c. distraction, d. indigenous, e. ascetic.

1. Woody Allen has been making people laugh by playing a single character who is so _____ , so human and so chummy that his fans feel they have an intimate personal relationship with him.

2. He is serious in the sense that he tries hard to live the _____ life of an artist rather than the public life of an entertainer.

3. "I've always felt I was _____ as a filmmaker on the basis of triviality."

4. He doesn't look at art as a solution to the dread of death—but at least making movies is a _____ .

5. "The type of drama that interests me most is not _____ to the United States."

5 points for each correct answer   SCORE: _____

II. MAIN IDEA

Put an M next to the two statements that express the main ideas of the selection.

_____ **1.** Allen believes in hard work and accomplishment.

_____ **2.** It is important for Woody Allen to deal with serious matters of life in both his comedy and his films.

_____ **3.** Woody Allen enjoys his slapstick image.

_____ **4.** Death is a subject with which Allen has come to terms only after extensive reading and research.

20 points for each correct answer   SCORE: _____

III. CHARACTERIZATION

Put a check ✓ next to five words that would describe Woody Allen

_____ **1.** resolute   _____ **5.** concerned
_____ **2.** relaxed   _____ **6.** motivated
_____ **3.** lighthearted   _____ **7.** leisurely
_____ **4.** disciplined   _____ **8.** burdened

5 points for each correct answer   SCORE: _____

IV. CRITICAL THINKING

Circle the letter (a, b or c) that correctly completes the following sentences.

1. Discipline
   a. comes naturally at any age.
   b. requires effort and determination.
   c. is acquired with little work.

2. Woody Allen is determined because
   a. he enjoys the glory of stardom.
   b. he wants to be another Charlie Chaplin.
   c. of the importance of his messages.

5 points for each correct answer   SCORE: _____

PERFECT TOTAL SCORE: 100   TOTAL SCORE: _____

V. QUESTIONS FOR THOUGHT

Do you think it is dangerous for people to see entertainers only as the characters they play? Explain. Do you think the public is entitled to know the person behind the actor?

Notes from the <u>Real</u> Little House on the Prairie

Laura Ingalls Wilder

Laura Ingalls Wilder was the author of what is considered by many people to be the most acclaimed set of children's books ever written. They were and are universally popular with both critics and children alike. A television series based on these books was entitled *Little House on the Prairie*. It captured the loyal viewing interest of adults and children countrywide.

The first of the *Little House* books, as they came to be called, appeared in 1933 during the Depression. It was just what America craved, and Laura proceeded to write more. She was often asked how she came to write these stories of pioneer days. Shortly after she finished the volume entitled *On the Banks of Plum Creek*, she wrote this account in black pencil on lined paper—as Laura wrote almost everything.

Years ago, in the Little House in the Big Woods, sister Mary and I listened to Father's wonderful stories.

There was no radio to amuse us then, no moving pictures to go see, so when the day's work was done, we lingered in the twilight or sat by the evening lamp and listened intently to Pa's stories and the music of his violin. Our little family had to be self-sufficient for its own entertainment as well as its livelihood, and there was no lack of either.

Mother was of old Scottish ancestry and inherited the tra-

Laura Ingalls Wilder was a quiet and gentle woman who wrote of her respect and passion for frontier life.

We had a busy, happy childhood, but of it all, Sister Mary and I loved Pa's stories best. We never forgot them, and I have always felt they were too good to be altogether lost. Children today could not have a childhood like mine in the Big Woods of Wisconsin, but they could learn of it and hear the stories that Pa used to tell. But I put off writing them from year to year and was past 60 when I wrote my first book, *The Little House in the Big Woods*.

When to my utter astonishment the book made such a success and children from all over the United States wrote imploring me for more stories, I began to think what a wonderful childhood I had had, how I had experienced the whole frontier: the woods, the Indian country of the Great Plains, the frontier towns, the building of railroads in wild, unsettled country, homesteading, farmers arriving to take possession. I realized that I had witnessed it all—all the successive phases of the frontier, first the frontiersmen, then the pioneers, the farmers and the towns. Then I understood that in my own life I represented an entire period of American history. That the frontier was gone and agricultural settlements had taken its

ditional thriftiness that helped with the livelihood. Although born and bred on the frontier, she was an educated, cultured woman. She was very quiet and gentle, but proud and particular in all matters of good breeding.

Father's ancestors arrived in America on the *Mayflower* and he was born in New York State. But he also was raised on the frontier. He was always jolly though inclined to be reckless, and he loved his violin.

So Ma taught us books and trained us in our manners, while Pa taught us other things and entertained us.

Pioneers on the frontier encountered raging winds and torrential rain storms.

place when I married a farmer. It seemed to me that my childhood had been much richer and more interesting than that of children today, even with all the modern inventions and improvements.

I wanted the children now to understand more about the beginnings of things, to know what is behind the things they see—what it is that made America as they know it. Then I thought of writing the story of my childhood in several books—an eight-volume historical novel for children covering every aspect of the American frontier.

After the work was well started, I was told that such a thing had never been done before—that a novel of several volumes was only for grown-ups. My daughter, Rose Wilder Lane, a writer and novelist, said it would be unique.

I hesitated. Perhaps my idea was all wrong.

But letters kept coming from children, individuals, whole classes in schools, parents of children too small to write letters—all wanted to know what happened next, wanted me to go on with the story. I decided to do so. Someone has to do a thing first; I would be the first

Homesteaders in areas like Minnesota and the Dakota Territory built rough cabins to help withstand hard winters.

to write a multivolume novel for children. So I wrote the second volume, *Farmer Boy*. This is the story of Almanzo, a farm boy in the East before he went west. It is the story of the childhood of my husband on his father's farm, near Malone, New York.

The third volume of my children's novel, *The Little House on the Prairie*, goes back again to Laura as does the fourth volume, *On the Banks of Plum*

Creek, just finished.

Almanzo, the farmer boy, appears again in the fifth volume on which I am now working. He goes with Laura the rest of the way through the three more volumes it will take to make the eight and complete the novel. But these are still to be written, so I'll not give any details now.

On the Banks of Plum Creek features Laura and her family in western Minnesota where Ma was convinced they'd all be safe in a civilized country where nothing adverse could happen to them. She was an optimistic woman. When you read the book you will see how wrong she was. There were runaways and fires and storms—such terrible storms—and the grasshopper plague of 1874, the most devastating since the plagues of Egypt.

Even so, Plum Creek was too civilized for Pa, and we went west again to Dakota Territory where Almanzo was homesteading, where he helped save Laura and the other people of the new settlement from starving during the hard winter. And where he and Laura thought that zero weather was fine for sleighing but decided that 40 below was just a little too cold.

But that will all be told in the remaining volumes of my children's novel which ends happily (as all good novels should) when Laura of the *Little House* books and Almanzo of *Farmer Boy* were married.

Every story in this novel— each circumstance and each incident—is true. All I have told is true, though not the whole truth. There were some stories I wanted to tell but could not put in a book for children, even though I knew them as a child.

There was the story of the Bender family that belonged in *The Little House on the Prairie.* The Benders lived halfway between it and Independence, Kansas. We stopped there on our way to the Little House. Pa watered the horses and brought us all a drink from the well near the door of the house. I saw Kate Bender standing in the doorway. We did not go in because we could not afford to stop at a tavern.

On his trip to Independence to sell his furs, Pa stopped again for water, but did not go in for the same reason as before.

There were Kate Bender and her two brothers in the family, and their tavern was the only place for travelers to stop on the road south from Independence. People disappeared on

Family portrait of television show, "Little House on the Prairie"

that road. Leaving Independence and going south, they were never heard of again. It was thought that they were killed in the wilderness, but no bodies were ever found.

Then it was noticed that the Benders' garden was always freshly plowed but never planted. People wondered. And then a man came from the East looking for his missing brother.

He made up a party in Independence, and they followed the road south, but when they came to the Bender place no one was there. There were signs of hurried departure, and they searched the place.

The front room was partitioned by a calico curtain against which the dining table stood. On the curtain in the back of the table were stains about as high as the head of a man when seated. Behind the curtain was a trapdoor in the floor, and beside it lay a heavy hammer.

In the cellar underneath was the body of a man whose head had been crushed by the hammer. A grave was partly dug in the garden with a shovel close by. The posse searched the garden and dug up human bones and bodies. The garden was truly a graveyard kept plowed so it would show no signs of having been tampered with. The night of the day the bodies were found a neighbor rode up to our house and talked earnestly with Pa. We were never sure of what was said. But, then, Pa took his rifle down from its place over the door and said to Ma, "The vigilantes are called out." Then he saddled a horse and rode away with the neighbor.

It was late the next day when he came back. He never told us where he had been.

For several years there were occasional hunts for the Benders and reports that they had been seen here or there. At such times Pa always said in a strange tone of finality, "They will never be found." He knew. They never were found, and later I formed my own conclusions why.

You will agree it is not a fit story for a children's book. But it shows there were many dangers on the frontier, some for which people paid with their lives.

Sister Mary and I knew of these things but somehow were shielded from the full terror of them. Although we knew them to be true, they seemed unreal to us, for Ma was always there serene and quiet and Pa was there with his fiddle and his songs.

Laura and her husband Almanzo after their marriage in 1885

My parents possessed the frontier spirit. It was in their cheerfulness and humor. It shines through all the volumes of my novel.

Whether it was the Indian troubles or the terrible storms and the grasshoppers in Plum Creek, once past they looked ahead to better things.

When times were hard, Pa played the fiddle and sang—

Oh drive dull care away
For weeping is but sorrow.
If things are wrong today
There's another day tomorrow.

Number of Words: 1718 ÷ _____ Minutes Reading Time = Rate _____

I. SUMMARY

Put a check ✓ next to three statements that would be important to include in a summary of this selection.

_____ **1.** Laura Ingalls Wilder wrote an eight-volume novel for children about herself, her family, her friends and their lives and adventures in the frontier.

_____ **2.** Wilder asked her daughter for her opinion about writing a multivolume children's novel.

_____ **3.** The first Little House book was published in 1933 during the Depression and was instantly accepted and enjoyed by parents and children alike.

_____ **4.** Laura's series spans the successive phases of the frontier, as did her life, and it exemplifies the dangers as well as the joys of frontier life.

_____ **5.** Laura's husband, Almanzo, still loves horses, but now he drives a new car instead.

10 points for each correct answer   SCORE: _____

II. FACT/OPINION

Put an F next to each statement of fact and an O next to each sentence that expresses an opinion.

_____ **1.** The frontier was a difficult place in which to survive.

_____ **2.** Pa's stories were too good to be altogether lost.

_____ **3.** The first of the Little House books appeared in 1933.

_____ **4.** My childhood had been much richer and more interesting than that of children today even with all the modern inventions and improvements.

5 points for each correct answer   SCORE: _____

III. REFERENCE

Put a check ✓ next to five sources from which you could gain additional information about the land, people and events of the frontier.

_____	**1.**	historians	_____ **6.**	*Familiar Quotations*
_____	**2.**	scientific journals	_____ **7.**	history books
_____	**3.**	dictionary	_____ **8.**	*Dictionary of*
_____	**4.**	magazines		*American*
_____	**5.**	encyclopedias		*Biography*

5 points for each correct answer   SCORE: _____

IV. STORY ELEMENTS

Put a check ✓ next to the five words that describe the mood of Laura's account.

_____	**1.**	satisfied	_____ **5.**	proud
_____	**2.**	resentful	_____ **6.**	disillusioned
_____	**3.**	unhappy	_____ **7.**	fulfilled
_____	**4.**	sensitive	_____ **8.**	respectful

5 points for each correct answer   SCORE: _____

PERFECT TOTAL SCORE: 100   TOTAL SCORE: _____

V. QUESTIONS FOR THOUGHT

Why might Laura Ingalls Wilder believe that her childhood was probably much richer and more interesting than those of the children today? Do you agree with her? Why or why not?

Courage

Richard Filbin got to the station house at about 11:30 on a Saturday night in March. The deputy had the midnight-to-8 a.m. shift and didn't like to cut it too close.

He was changing into his uniform when Bob Hernandez walked over.

"How are you doing, Richard?" asked the 16-year-old Explorer Scout.

"I'll be better after a cup of coffee," answered the 26-year-old deputy good naturedly, despite his slight case of midnight grogginess.

He liked Bob and had gone on patrol with him many times before. The youngster was one of the police-officer trainees who serve in various branches of the Sheriff's Department as unpaid volunteers. It's a program run by the Explorer Scouts, and the hope is that the participants will eventually go on to become full-fledged deputy sheriffs.

Bob had already been at it for a year, and right from the beginning had fitted well into the station-house life. All the deputies treated him with admiration and good fellowship. Bob respected their profession, and to the deputies he represented its next generation.

on the Beat
Geraldo Rivera

Of all the officers assigned to the precinct, Bob preferred riding with Richard Filbin. The deputy was a friendly and helpful teacher and, even more important to Bob, he was a good cop.

Richard got a container of coffee from the machine and walked out of the lounge area. Bob walked alongside him to the briefing room.

"Can I ride with you tonight?" Bob asked Richard as they meandered down the long fluorescent-lit hallway.

"Sure, partner," the deputy answered with a smile, giving his young companion the kind of gentle pat on the back that means something like "Need you even ask!"

Once in the briefing room, the men of the midnight-to-eight shift all sat at one of the long tables facing the sergeant's podium. They sipped their coffee or told jokes until the superior officer called them to order and gave them a briefing that outlined the major crimes or other extraordinary situations currently affecting their assigned area. Bob took notes on almost everything the sergeant said. He took everything about the business of police work seriously.

Bob had aspired to become a policeman from the time he was in grade school. On the day he turned 15 he had become an Explorer Scout in the sheriff's special program.

After a rigorous training period, similar in most respects to the training of rookie officers, the boys in the program were allowed to function almost as deputies. They went out on patrol, used the two-way radios, took complaints and issued traffic tickets. Their uniforms were virtually the same as the deputies', and the only real difference was that the Scouts weren't permitted to carry any weapons.

The briefing lasted 15 minutes. When it was over, the deputies all walked back toward the front desk to grab their helmets and the large tin boxes they carried with them on patrol. The boxes were filled with things like the forms needed to make out the various reports, extra ammunition and a couple of alerts containing the pictures and descriptions of certain fugitives.

Richard and Bob had been assigned car 55B. When they got to the car, Bob put the tin box on the front seat, then did the "walkaround" with his partner. In the same way that pilots of small planes walk around and inspect their aircraft before takeoff, deputies are required to carefully check out their cars before going out on patrol.

After making the check, Deputy Filbin and Scout Hernandez pulled their car out of the parking lot and drove slowly out through the same double gate Richard had entered a half-hour before.

Saturday-night patrols always had more than their share of sticky situations. This one started with a call to check on a large drunk-and-disorderly party. The appearance of the slowly cruising patrol car had the desired calming effect. Bob and Rich didn't even have to get out of their car.

When the loitering kids they spotted turned out to be very young neighborhood boys, the deputy decided to let them off with a warning.

A heart-attack emergency shortly followed. Summoned to the scene, Deputy Filbin applied first-aid resuscitation, while Bob kept the curious away from the victim until the ambulance arrived.

"It's been a busy hour," the deputy said to Bob after they

had resumed their patrolling.

"Yeah . . . but we don't have much to show for it," complained the 16-year-old.

Whenever they patrolled together, Richard would act as a tutor, discussing hypothetical police problems with his receptive protégé. Once Bob had finished describing what he would do in certain imaginary situations, the deputy would point out the flaws, if any, in Bob's answer.

Tonight's lesson was simply to be patient.

"You know," Richard continued, "sometimes the busiest nights, and the nights you do your best police work, are the ones when you don't make a single arrest. . . .

Just then the radio burst alive. Deputy Donald Bear in car 55A was requesting assistance. It wasn't an immediate emergency. The deputy was in the process of arresting somebody when an angry crowd started gathering around him.

Filbin picked up the microphone and said, "This is car 55B . . . car 55B, please advise car 55A that our ETA is in two minutes. Repeating, car 55B responding. Our estimated time of arrival, Parlin Street, is two minutes."

Deputy Bear had been patrolling when he noticed a

group of about six noisy young men standing on the lawn in front of a house, looking suspicious. The deputy pulled over to question the group, but just as he was getting out of the patrol car, they broke and ran, most of them disappearing into the house.

Chasing the others on foot, Bear had managed to grab one of the men he'd allegedly seen with some stolen goods.

In any case, as he was escorting the man back toward the patrol car, the others came back out of the house and followed menacingly behind him. A couple of very angry older men had joined them, and the new additions were obviously drunk.

"Where're you takin' him?"

"You ain't goin' nowhere with Jimmy."

When Bear got to the car, he pushed the trouble-maker against the vehicle and ordered him to put his hand on the roof. But the rest of the group, staring morosely, formed a tightening semicircle around the deputy and continued to shout their insulting challenges and seemingly were waiting to spring out at him.

That was when Bear had radioed for a backup unit, vigilant against turning his back on the crowd when he was doing it.

He recognized others from the original group and decided to grab them also when help finally arrived.

Car 55B decelerated as soon as it entered the street. Deputy Filbin had gotten there as quickly as he could, but the last thing he wanted to do now was upset a potentially explosive situation with a dramatic arrival.

Driving casually down the street, he and Bob could see the other deputy's car parked farther up on the left-hand side.

Richard parked behind that car and started walking toward the standoff; Bob was alongside him.

"Hey, Bob," the deputy said softly, "this doesn't look all that good. You better call for some more help."

"Right," the 16-year-old answered as he hurried back to the patrol car. Richard continued on, until he was close enough to ask Deputy Bear what was happening. When Bear had finished his quick, whispered explanation, Richard gave the group a hard look. Bear had pointed out the others who'd been involved in the incident, and the two deputies started walking toward them.

But as they approached, the boisterous group started backing up toward the house again.

Those who'd been involved in the original group had already gone inside the house by the time the deputies got up to the porch. The older man was blocking the door.

"Step aside, sir," ordered Deputy Bear.

"Where's your search warrant?" slurred the drunk who was evidently the owner of the house.

Filbin was on the porch, standing on the right; Bear was alongside, to the left; Bob, who had rejoined them after sending the call for help, was at the foot of the steps between the two of them.

"We're in the process of making a felony arrest, sir," explained Filbin. The provocation was getting to him. "We don't need a warrant."

At this point the deputies were just trying to bide their time until additional help arrived. Bear actually had his foot in the door. When he forced it momentarily open, he could see one of the suspects. He pointed at him, telling Filbin that he was the guy they really wanted.

"C'mon out," Deputy Filbin ordered.

The young man walked into the center of the living room, crossed his arms and smiled. "Come and take me," he said.

Filbin began vainly pushing against the door, trying to assist Deputy Bear in his efforts to keep it open. Then differences really mounted. The group at the door started kicking and shoving. Somebody grabbed for Bear's holster and almost got it unstrapped. But Bob, standing just behind him, managed to knock the hand away.

The outnumbered deputies were definitely getting the worst of a bad situation. Bear had been shoved twice, and both Bob and Richard had taken several blows to the face. Finally, with perseverance, they were able to drive their attackers back inside the house.

Then the first shot was fired. Deputy Filbin described it as "a flashcube going off from the middle of the crowd." The sound of it was deafening, drowning out the memory of the shouting that had immediately preceded it. It momentarily stunned the deputies.

Filbin turned to look at his 16-year-old partner. The kid looked shocked. "I'm hit!" he told Rich.

Bob was knocked completely off the porch by the force of the bullet. Lying against a car in the driveway, he had been hit in the thigh; blood was pumping out.

"Help!" shouted Filbin.

Bang. Another shot, a half-second later, twisted Deputy Bear around and also threw him off the little porch. Bang. Filbin flew into the air. He hit against the wall to his right, then crashed against the ground. His legs were paralyzed.

Just then, the house door slammed shut.

Crumpled against the car in the driveway, Bob felt "like my whole leg had been torn off." He was watching when Deputy Filbin got taken down.

"I was holding my leg to slow the blood down," Bob remembers, "trying to decide if I should just fall down and forget about the whole thing."

Watching Richard go down got Bob moving again. Somehow he managed to drag him-

self over to the patrol car, parked about 30 feet (9.14 meters) away. He struggled to get the door open, but it took time because his hands were slippery with blood. When he finally managed it, he fell across the front seat and lost consciousness.

Bang! Another shot brought him back. He grabbed the radio.

"Car 55B requesting code-three assistance . . . car 55B requesting code-three assistance!" Code three demands immediate response from all available units, with sirens and lights.

"Code 999! Code 999!" he shouted into the radio. The signal means that officers have been hit in a shooting. It's the highest priority call, the police equivalent to a "Mayday!"

Barbara, the night dispatcher, was on the desk. Trying to keep cool, she had forced her voice to be calm when she answered. "Car 55B, this is dispatcher. Assistance is on the way."

Then Bob groped for the shotgun, and only with great difficulty managed to pry it from its rack under the front seat. Then the 16-year-old Explorer started squirming out of the car, his exit made easier than his entrance by the blood now covering the seat.

Holding the shotgun, he stood up uncertainly and staggered toward the house. He managed to reach the car parked in the house driveway. He propped his elbows against its hood and pointed the shotgun at the door. Filbin was still lying on the ground, and he wasn't moving. Bear was sitting under one of the house windows. He had taken Filbin's gun and fired a fifth round into the door to keep the people away.

Even that close to him, Bob thought Filbin had been killed. Suddenly his partner moaned, "Please . . . somebody help me. . . ."

"Hang on, Rich. You'll be all right," Bob called out to him.

"Bob. Can you get Rich out of there?" asked Bear, who was on the other side of Filbin.

"I can't!" Bob shouted back. "I'm hit bad in the leg, and I don't know how long I'll last!"

"Cover the door," Bear replied. "I'll try it!"

Deputy Bear ran hunched over, so he wouldn't be seen from the windows. As he ran, he held his bleeding hand against his chest. He reached Filbin, grabbed him under the arms and, despite the pain in his hand, started dragging him toward the street.

"If the door opens . . . blow it!" Bear shouted to Bob.

"I will!" the 16-year-old replied loudly enough so the people inside could hear him. He was standing now in a pool of his own blood.

Somebody pulled the curtains aside in the living-room window.

"Stay away from that window!" Bob shouted as he aimed the shotgun. He could still hear Filbin moaning as Bear reached the street.

"How is he?" he called out to Bear.

"Don't worry about him . . . watch the door!"

"I'm bleeding bad. I won't be able to stand here much longer."

"Hang on, kid." Bob maintained his vigil, weakening every moment. Finally a car arrived.

It skidded to a stop in front of the house, and two deputies jumped out.

"Get Filbin to a hospital!" or-

dered Deputy Bear.

With the driver of the car helping, they managed to get him into the front seat, and the car took off. The other deputy from that car stayed. Also armed with a shotgun, he took up a position next to Bob behind the car in the driveway.

"You all right?" the deputy asked the 16-year-old next to him.

"I'm hit. In the leg." The kid was obviously about to collapse.

"Go ahead. Try to get to the street. I'll cover the house."

As Bob worked his way toward the safety of the street, he could hear the sirens of at least a half-dozen patrol cars rapidly approaching.

Within minutes, Parlin Street was filled by patrol cars parked randomly all over the place. Shouting men, wearing bulletproof vests, were running toward the house with shotguns, and almost all the residents of Parlin Street were

standing out on the lawns in front of their houses, watching.

Bob had collapsed in the gutter.

Deputy Bear grabbed the driver of another recently arrived patrol car.

"You got to get me and the kid out of here!" he told the deputy who was driving. The men inside jumped out and carried Bob to the car.

Within minutes he was on one of the tables in the Garfield Hospital Emergency Room.

Word quickly spread around the hospital that a 16-year-old hero had just been admitted. A doctor walked in and asked him how he was doing.

"I'm bleeding pretty bad. . . . Can you stop it?"

The doctor examined him, told him exactly where the wound was and started cutting his pants off.

"No! Don't cut them. The detectives will want to see them," Bob advised. "Let's just take them off."

As the doctor took off Bob's left boot to get his clothes off, blood dripped out.

A nurse came in and asked Bob whom he'd like them to contact. Bob asked them to get in touch with his mother, then changed his mind and asked if he could call her. That wasn't permitted, so Bob gave the nurse his brother's phone number. He didn't want his mom finding out from a stranger.

Bob's 29-year-old brother, Andy, was the first one there.

"Hi, bro!" Bob greeted him with studied nonchalance.

"How are you?"

"I'm okay."

"Sure you are."

His sister Anita, brother Danny and his mother all arrived together. His mother ran over to him and embraced him, crying and asking if he was all right. Bob told them that he was fine, but as he spoke they could see blood seeping through the sheet the nurses had thrown over him. He asked everybody who came into his room about Richard, and everybody told him that his partner was doing fine.

A couple of hours after he had arrived at the hospital, Bob was wheeled into surgery. It had taken that long before the young hero could be treated because the operating room was being used for Deputy Filbin. He was being brought out as Bob was wheeled in.

The last thing Bob remembered before being knocked out for the operation was a doctor telling him not to worry. "You'll both be home in a couple of days."

For his actions, Bob was awarded the Honor Medal with crossed palms. It's the highest award the Boy Scouts of America, of which the Explorers are a part, can present. He also received a law-enforcement award from the federal government and the distinguished-service award of the Sheriff's Department.

In a special ceremony, attended by several high-ranking county officials, Sheriff Peter Pitchess said, "During these times, when the demands on law enforcement are ever increasing, Robert's actions reflect great credit upon today's youth, and it gives me great pleasure to extend our appreciation by honoring this outstanding young man."

Number of Words: 2948 ÷ _____ Minutes Reading Time = Rate _____

I. CHARACTERIZATION

Put a check √ next to the three words under the name of each character that best describe him.

1. Robert Hernandez
    _____ **a.** greedy   _____ **d.** adventurous
    _____ **b.** courageous   _____ **e.** arrogant
    _____ **c.** self-centered   _____ **f.** persevering

2. Richard Filbin
    _____ **a.** sensitive   _____ **d.** weak
    _____ **b.** crude   _____ **e.** evasive
    _____ **c.** brave   _____ **f.** calm

5 points for each correct answer   SCORE: _____

II. PROBLEM SOLVING

Circle the letter (a, b or c) that tells how the characters in the story solved the following problems:

1. Deputy Filbin was lying in the open, wounded.
    a. Hernandez and Bear waited for reinforcements.
    b. Bear moved Filbin while Hernandez covered him.
    c. The officers surrendered to the angry mob.

2. The deputies were hurt and outnumbered.
    a. Bob fired a round into the house through the door.
    b. Bob pulled Bear and Filbin to the safety of the car.
    c. Bob dragged himself to the car and radioed for help.

3. A large party had become drunk and disorderly.
    a. Bob requested the group to quiet down.
    b. The deputies drove by the house slowly enough to be seen.
    c. Filbin issued a summons to the owner of the house.

10 points for each correct answer   SCORE: _____

III. CLASSIFYING

Put a check √ next to two actions that show courage.

_____ **1.** The deputy let the loitering kids off with a warning.

_____ **2.** Bob dragged himself 30 feet over to the patrol car, his leg bleeding furiously, to call for help.

_____ **3.** Bob flung the license into the driver's window.

_____ **4.** Bob staggered toward the house, aiming a shotgun at the front door.

10 points for each correct answer   SCORE: _____

IV. AUTHOR'S PURPOSE

Put a check √ next to the statement that best tells the author's purpose for writing this selection.

_____ **1.** to show that the new generation possesses the qualities of courage and determination

_____ **2.** to deny that police work involves skill, tact and good judgment

_____ **3.** to show that a senior citizen can be brave and level-headed

20 points for correct answer   SCORE: _____

PERFECT TOTAL SCORE: 100   TOTAL SCORE: _____

V. QUESTIONS FOR THOUGHT

Should peer pressure be the ultimate factor in decision making? Why or why not?

School for Elephants

Denis D. Gray

"Soooong!" shouts the chief of mahouts. As quickly and nimbly as pointer dogs, a dozen elephants lift their right forelegs and 12 mahouts (riders and keepers of elephants in Asia for generations) swing up to lodge themselves behind huge flapping ears and powerful necks. Two younger animals, a good 800 pounds (362 kilograms) apiece, crack each other playfully on the head, oblivious to the sounds of crisp, morning discipline. An older elephant scoops up a bouquet of branches and deftly swats at the flies buzzing around its skin.

It is two hours after sunrise at the Young Elephants Training Center in northern Thailand—two hours after the "students" have lumbered out of the hilly jungle surrounding the school to be scrubbed down in a mountain pool and preened for the morning's training. Today, like most days, these elephants will practice pulling teak logs with chains strapped to their massive bodies. They will lift and stack logs weighing a ton or so into neat piles with their tusks, and they will work through an impressive repertoire of some 26 commands. "The oldest student here is ten," says Nuon Komrue, the chief of mahouts. "He will graduate soon and go to work in the teak forests."

Meanwhile, 330 miles (530.97 kilometers) to the south in the bustling Thai capital of Bangkok, a sales executive points to a yellow, 20-foot-long piece of machinery with a stubby blade up front, a powerful winch in the back and four massive, deep-tread tires. The tractor-

Elephants are scrubbed down in a mountain pool and readied for school.

like, American-made vehicle is called a "skidder." The salesman ticks off its advantages: a medium-size skidder can pull logs weighing up to 20 tons; a full-grown elephant can manage no more than two tons. Like an elephant, the machine can climb precarious slopes and swivel around trees. It takes three to four days to train a skidder driver, while elephant schooling lasts about seven years. And the skidder, moving faster than an elephant, never tires. True, a medium model skidder costs about $75,000 while a fully trained elephant in Thailand currently fetches some $4,000, but in the long run the machine pulls ahead in cost effectiveness. The executive says that 250 units of his company's model have been sold in Thailand, and the demand rises year by year.

Only a few decades ago, local foresters and European teak dealers would invariably have concluded that elephants were "the most lovable and wise of all beasts." Able to move up slopes of as much as 70 degrees, push through thick jungle and break up log jams in

A high-riding mahout and his elephant

rivers and streams with powerful head and trunk thrusts, the elephants made possible a multimillion dollar industry in remote stretches of Asia during the 19th century and the first half of the 20th. Consequently, they were pampered, doctored and normally loved by the men who had spent much of their lives with them in the forests of India, Burma, Thailand and elsewhere. Now the Thai skidder salesman predicts that it is only a matter of time before machinery will totally replace elephants as logging workers in Thailand, and eventually in all of Asia.

Is the age of the elephant industry really passing? The statistics seem to say so. In Thailand the domestic elephant population has dropped, according to government statistics, some 5000 since the end of World War II. And in Burma there are now some 2700 working elephants compared with about 5200 employed by British and other foreign firms before the war.

The Asian elephant—lighter and smaller than its African cousin—runs wild in India, Burma, Thailand, Vietnam, Laos, Cambodia, Indonesia, Sri Lanka, Malaysia, Nepal, China, Bangladesh and possibly other

Elephants, large and small, at the start of the annual Elephant Roundup Show in northeast Thailand

areas. An Asian elephant-study group estimated the wild population to be between 34,000 and 45,000. But at a meeting called to discuss the situation, trouble was predicted. One conference paper even warned that wild elephants in Thailand would be seriously threatened with extinction within a decade.

But at least one member of the study group, Jeffrey A. McNeely, an American conservationist who has worked in Thailand for almost a decade, believes that the elephant, as a working animal, still has a future in an energy-short world.

"Elephants run on local fuel, reproduce themselves and still can go into some places that machines can't," he says. Elephants are going to be around longer than petroleum. They've also shown an amazing ability to adapt to encroaching civilization in Asia.

Certainly the training school for young elephants in Thailand seems unfazed by dire predictions. Here, the centuries-old bond between man and elephant still exists. With less than 100 pounds on his frame, Nuon Komrue is dwarfed by the animals around him, but they are his life. The chief mahout says he has worked daily with them for 22 of his 49 years, ever since he traded his pans and ladles for a bull hook. The son of a poor rice farmer, Nuon started as a cook for the Forest Industry Organization, the government department that runs the school. Taking a liking to the animals, he talked his way into a job as a *Khon Teen*—a foot-person charged with performing some of the more menial tasks of elephant care without actually being allowed to ride the animals. He became a mahout two years later.

Although some groups in Thailand—especially a few tribes living along the Cambodian border—have been elephant men (there are no women mahouts) for generations, those at the school and others in northern Thailand come from varied backgrounds and don't necessarily pass on their skill to their offspring.

Slight, with whiskers and a wispy beard, Nuon smiles broadly as he describes his life.

A veteran mahout with some of the beasts he has tended and taught for much of his life

He rises daily at five except on Buddhist holidays—days of the full and half-moon—when the school is closed. He eats a bowl of sticky rice, sometimes graced with bamboo shoots or other vegetables from his garden. Then he strides into the forest with the other mahouts to locate the school's students, who are let out to feed and rest each night.

It's about an hour's walk, but Nuon says it isn't any trouble finding the herd. The men know their own animals so well that they can track them down by the characteristics of their droppings or the grass and leaves they chew and then spit out by the wayside.

"Phe, phe," the mahouts call out to the elephants. "Come, come." Dutifully, the elephants saunter out of the thick green to their masters, ready to be mounted and ridden out of the jungle to the school.

The school is the only one of its kind in Thailand, and it has built an enviable academic record as far as most educational institutions go. It has never had a dropout and its director, Dr. Chaum Kinvudhi, says he can't remember teaching a stupid student.

While private entrepreneurs, villagers and some tribes in Thailand still catch wild elephants and train them without benefit of "formal schooling," the school's recruits come from the 100 or so animals that work for the Forest Industry Organization, which operates various logging sites around the country. A pregnant mother from one of these sites is put on a 10-wheeled, specially cushioned truck and ferried to the school in time to give birth to a baby that automatically becomes enrolled. The baby stays with its mother at the school for three years or so and then undergoes what the mahouts describe as a painful separation. The mother goes back to work in the forest, and the child begins a training program that will last for the next seven years.

The young elephant is placed in a tight pen made of logs and with the help of sugarcane and other elephant delicacies is taught the basic commands. It also becomes familiar with hobbles and dragging gear, and with having a mahout perched on its back. The school director says that the elephants can pick up the basic commands in two weeks to a month.

Out of the pen, the elephant spends the next year in the basics of logging work and a daily routine on the training ground:

walking in file and in pairs, stopping, getting down on all fours, lifting and pulling. The commands are shouted out by the mahouts in a combination of Thai, a local Thai dialect and the language of the Karen, the great elephant keepers of Burma and Thailand. Each verbal command also has its equivalent in a subtle, if not gentle-seeming, kick, rub or knee thrust by the mahout in the region of the elephant's ears and neck. On command, a column of elephants will wheel around in sharp precision, and a bull elephant will thrust his tusks under a log and start lifting without a sound being uttered.

Teamwork, the director says, is the most difficult part of the training but elephants seem to come by it naturally. In the wild, elephants have been seen to sandwich a baby between them as protection against tigers or, working as a pair, to ferry a young one across a swift stream by using their trunks as rafts. When a mother gives birth, a companion, called an "auntie," is on hand to act as midwife, tearing off the membrane in which the 200-pound baby comes, and helping the newborn in beginning its breast-feeding.

The teamwork at the school is designed to get as much elephant muscle behind a certain task as possible. A heavy log may be chained to two or more elephants, who heave in unison. Or a trio of animals may move up on a log, scoop it up simultaneously with their tusks and lay it gently on a pile, taking care that no member of the team gets ahead or behind another member.

After passing through primary and secondary training at the school, the elephant, aged about 10 or 11, is ready for work on one of the government's forestry projects, hauling sawed logs from timber sites through the jungle to yards from which the logs are transported by trucks, train or water to the markets. This is the battleground between the elephants and the more sophisticated logging machines.

Both during training and in work the elephants labor only a few hours a day and then are let out to roam and gorge themselves with their daily intake of vegetation and as much as 50 gallons of water. There are weekly rest days, and from March until May the elephants are brought to a "summer vacation camp" during which they do nothing but feed, sleep and mate. Retirement is mandatory, and medical care for sensitive animals is prompt and professional.

A mahout will normally take the same elephant through training and move with it after graduation. The pair may stay together for decades. "You speak to them like you would to a person," says one mahout from atop his animal. "You say things like, 'You have to be a good girl. Now, why are you doing this?' After all, I brought up this elephant."

The retired elephant, like the expectant mother, returns to the school. A mahout is assigned to do nothing but take care of its needs. Today, there are two retired elephants at the school, both in their late sixties. They live in the forest, and the mahouts visit them every two or three days. The two feed themselves, wandering through the forest along with deer, wild boar, squirrels, snakes and other animals. They will sleep three to four hours during the course of a day, lying down on their flanks, yawning and snoring like humans.

The mahouts look after the

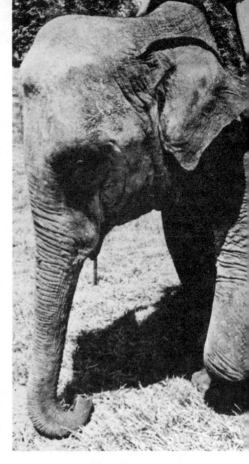

retired elephants' skin sores and other hurts. They bring bundled sticks of sugarcane, bananas and the elephants' favorites: sweet-sour pods of tamarind, wrapped up in a ball with a globule of salt inside. The mahouts continue coming into the jungle until one day their charges sink down to the forest floor for their last, long sleep.

Number of Words: 2003 ÷ _____ Minutes Reading Time = Rate _____

I. SKIMMING

Answer the questions by circling the correct letter (a, b or c).

1. How many animals work for the Forest Industry
   Organization?
   a. 100   **b.** 4000   **c.** 500

2. What is the American-made vehicle for logging called?
   a. a winch   **b.** a skidder   **c.** a tractor

3. Where is the Young Elephants Training Center located?
   a. India   **b.** Burma   **c.** Thailand

4. What is the most difficult part of elephant training?
   a. primary school
   b. taming
   c. teamwork

5 points for each correct answer   SCORE: _____

II. MAIN IDEA

Place a check √ before the two sentences that state the main ideas in this story.

_____ **1.** Elephants enjoy sweet-sour pods of tamarind with
         their meals.

_____ **2.** Modern machinery is beginning to replace the
         elephants.

_____ **3.** Elephants at the Training School learn how to obey.

_____ **4.** The elephant is an integral part of Thailand's
         culture.

_____ **5.** Elephant School prepares its students for circus life.

10 points for each correct answer   SCORE: _____

III. SEQUENCE

Number the following statements from 1 to 6, according to the order in which they appear in the selection.

_____ **a.** Retirement is mandatory at age 60 for an elephant of the Forest Organization.

_____ **b.** Logging work and a daily routine are taught to the elephant on the training ground.

_____ **c.** At age 10 or 11 the elephant is ready for work on one of the government forest projects.

_____ **d.** The elephant becomes familiar with gear and with carrying a mahout on its back.

_____ **e.** The elephant is taught to work in unison with his peers.

_____ **f.** The young elephant is placed in a tight pen, given delicacies and taught the basic commands.

10 points for each correct answer   SCORE: _____

PERFECT TOTAL SCORE: 100   TOTAL SCORE: _____

IV. QUESTIONS FOR THOUGHT

What are the differences between working with an animal and with a machine? Which do you think you'd prefer?

A Behind-the-Scenes

an Anchorwoman

Look at

Dolly Berry

There was a time when most young American girls dreamed of becoming nurses, teachers or homemakers. But dreams change, and currently many career-minded women are bypassing the hospital, classroom and kitchen in favor of the bright lights of the television studio. Their goal? Anchorwoman.

Beverly Williams is an excellent example. For the last four years, her home away from home has been TV station KYW-TV in Philadelphia. At 30, she is in the public eye in a seemingly glamorous role. Just how enviable this profession is, however, seems to depend a lot on which side of the camera you're on.

10:30 a.m.

The banner on the wall asks "Where will the Instant Eye take you tonight?" Beverly Williams smiles when she sees it, then grimaces as she approaches her paper-laden desk. As she gulps a cup of coffee from a paper cup and munches a bite of stale sweet roll, the telephone announces the first of many calls. Lifting the receiver to her ear, Beverly assumes an air of total concentration and professionalism.

Anchorwoman Beverly Williams reworking her notes in a TV script.

11:00 a.m.
To prepare herself for the noon news broadcast, Beverly must familiarize herself with the stories that were "hot" last night. Much of her preliminary work in updating the news for the first telecast of the day is done by phone. "How many men were involved in the corruption scandal? When will the blockade be lifted from the radical headquarters? Is that warehouse fire believed to be arson?" Fingers crouched over the typewriter keys, she reworks her quickly jotted notes into a script for the noon news.

Producer Don Shoultz motions for Bev to join him and co-anchorperson Roy Weissinger at the assignment board. The three of them decide which story will fit best into which segment of the news, where live minicam shots should be used, whether an auto accident is too gory to be shown and whether the Ben Vereen tape can be edited in time to make the 12:25 segment.

11:15 a.m.
Pushing the cold dregs of her coffee out of the way, Bev resumes the writing of her script. Within seconds of the completion of her first story the clattering teletype updates the story, rendering her script obsolete. Bev just shrugs as she aims

Beverly, getting a final briefing from some of the TV staff, before going on the air.

the crumpled yellow sheet of copy at the wastebasket. It's happened many times before . . . on to the next one.

11:40 a.m.
With only 20 minutes left before going on the air, Beverly dashes to the dressing table to apply "television makeup." As she deftly puts on theatrical pancake, her mind is racing ahead to her opening segment. Blusher and eyeshadow are brushed on mechanically as she rereads her script. A final fluff to her curls, a misting of hair spray, and it's eight minutes to air time. Lipstick in hand, she rushes for the elevator.

12:01 p.m.
There are three cameras focusing on Beverly as she reads her script from the teleprompter. She must be alert to every signal from the floor manager—as the red light comes on atop camera number two, Bev must turn toward that camera. She can relax for 30 seconds while Roy reads the next story but must be ready with the following one as soon as he finishes.

12:15 p.m.
The floor manager points a finger at Bev—her cue to wrap up the noon news. She tells the story of a little boy who was born with his heart outside his body. Surgeons at Philadel-

Final preparation for mid-day broadcast includes applying TV makeup.

phia's Children's Hospital were confident that the baby would soon be able to go home for the first time in his two and a half years of life. On that upbeat note, Bev signs off for Roy and herself. The noon news is over ... time now to get ready for the 6:00 broadcast.

1:05 p.m.

Bev receives word that there's been a bank robbery in a wealthy Philadelphia suburb. The robber has been wounded by police gunfire. Bev grabs her tape recorder and notebook and runs for the elevator. The Instant Eye van, with camera crew aboard, is already waiting for her on the corner.

2:00 p.m.

After maneuvering through heavy traffic, the Instant Eye finally pulls up in front of the bank. Bev is puzzled by the lack of activity. When she attempts to open the bank's front door she finds that it's locked. A small handwritten note taped to the window says: "Bank closed due to robbery. Please use one of our other branches." A white chalk outline on the sidewalk gives mute testimony—this is where the bank robber died. An eyewitness gives Bev a brief account of the holdup. The cameramen film the blood spots near the chalk outline.

No sooner is one telecast over than it's back out on another assignment.

3:45 p.m.
Back in the Instant Eye van, Bev monitors the police radio. Suddenly she hears a bulletin: A child has fallen onto the railroad tracks and is injured. Bev hears the police calling for an ambulance. The Instant Eye is only a mile from the scene.

Beverly hangs on as the cameraman careens in and out of traffic. She jumps down from the van even before it comes to a full stop at the scene of the accident. She spots a little boy crying in the arms of a policeman.

3:55 p.m.
While paramedics hurry the child into the ambulance, Beverly questions the good samaritan who found the frightened boy and summoned aid for him.

As the paramedics cut the shirt from the child's chest, Beverly listens intently to find out the specifics of what happened. The sobbing little boy explains that he was playing near the railroad tracks, lost his balance and fell onto a railway track.

4:35 p.m.
The Instant Eye speeds back toward the studio. Bev wants the story to make the 6:00 news.

She sprints into the Eyewitness newsroom and heads for the editing booth.

An assignment successfully completed, Beverly enjoys a happy moment.

5:15 p.m.

Scenes of the good samaritan, the little boy in the ambulance and the railroad tracks flash before Bev's eyes as the videotape is run in slow motion. She cuts here, does a voiceover there . . . but she's still not satisfied with the result.

With minutes to go before air time, Bev gives the tape to the producer. After padding back to her desk in her bare feet, she watches herself on the 6:00 news and notices that she was given credit for securing an exclusive.

7:00 p.m.

Beverly Williams has finished most of her paperwork. She's returned most of the calls that came in while she was out on assignment and answered most of her mail. Soon the air will heat up again in preparation for the 11:00 news. But for the moment Bev can breathe easy and go home for a few hours.

7:05 p.m.

The banner on the wall asks "Where will the Instant Eye take you tonight?" Beverly Williams knows the answer . . . She's been there.

Number of Words: 1138 ÷ _____ Minutes Reading Time = Rate _____

I. GENERALIZATIONS

Check three generalizations that could be made about the job of anchorperson.

_____ **1.** One must be versatile and adaptable.

_____ **2.** It requires good judgment and varied interests.

_____ **3.** It is a desk job.

_____ **4.** One must be efficient.

_____ **5.** Little training is needed to work in this position.

5 points for each correct answer   SCORE: _____

II. OUTLINING

Complete the outline by writing the letter of the following list of events in the proper places below, as they appear in the story.

a. writing news pieces
b. being aware of camera cues
c. covering live stories
d. returning calls

  I.   Preparations for a News Show Are Varied
       A. keeping abreast of latest news developments.
       B. _____
       C. editing and ordering the news show
       D. _____
 II.   Considerations During the News Show
       A. reading scripts from the teleprompter
       B. timing the reports so they flow
       C. _____
III.   Responsibilities After the News Show
       A. doing paperwork
       B. _____

10 points for each correct answer   SCORE: _____

III. CRITICAL THINKING

Circle the letter (a, b or c) that correctly completes each sentence.

1. Beverly Williams
    a. resents giving up so much of her time.
    b. gets satisfaction from her job.
    c. would rather be a newspaper reporter.

2. Women are entering the television news field because
    a. it is an easy way to earn a good living.
    b. it is less competitive than other fields.
    c. it is interesting and challenging.

15 points for each correct answer   SCORE: _____

IV. REFERENCE

Check ✓ the three sources from which you could find out about the requirements for getting a job on a television news show.

_____ **1.** a career counselor   _____ **4.** colleges or
_____ **2.** an atlas   universities
_____ **3.** television networks   _____ **5.** *Famous First
                                                              Facts*

5 points for each correct answer   SCORE: _____

PERFECT TOTAL SCORE: 100   TOTAL SCORE: _____

V. QUESTIONS FOR THOUGHT

Why haven't women been able to pursue such careers as anchor-person in the past? Do you know of any women who have gone into work traditionally done by men?

IN ADDITION TO LIFE AND LIMBS

Maya Pines

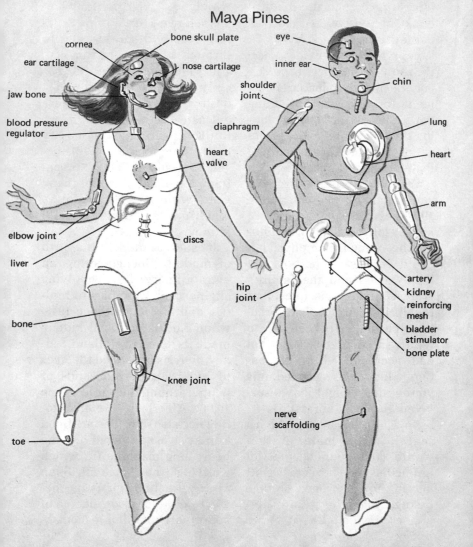

cornea — bone skull plate — eye

ear cartilage — nose cartilage — inner ear — chin

jaw bone — shoulder joint

blood pressure regulator — diaphragm — lung

heart valve — heart

liver — arm

elbow joint — discs — artery

hip joint — kidney

bone — reinforcing mesh

bladder stimulator

bone plate

knee joint

nerve scaffolding

toe

Laboratories use space-age technology to produce a new generation of artificial organs and synthetic body tissues.

A 19th-century English humorist once opened a medical book and discovered that he had every ailment in the book except for housemaid's knee. By the 21st century, a person may be able to order a replacement for almost every ailing part of his or her body, including the knee. That is the promise of a revolution which had its beginnings 40 years ago.

When Dr. Willem Kolff began practicing medicine in the 1930s, his first patient died of kidney failure. There was nothing the young Dutch physician could do to save the boy. His helplessness and the family's grief set him off on a quest that revolutionized medical practice. If he had only been able to remove some of the wastes that had accumulated in his patient's blood, he reasoned, this young man might have survived and led a normal life.

So Kolff began a stubborn search for a material that would contain blood, yet let impurities seep through. He hit on an unlikely one: sausage casings made of thin cellophane, then a new material.

When these casings were put in a salt solution, they became porous to many chemicals, but not to blood. Eventually Kolff built a device of cellophane tubes wrapped around a drum which was then partially immersed in a salt solution. A patient's blood could be run through the tubes and purified, a technique known as dialysis. Only the weakest and most desperately ill patients were entrusted to this device at first. But Kolff continued to modify the technique and patients began to respond. The 17th patient, a woman, lived for many years with the help of Kolff's machine—the first artificial kidney.

Its success marked the birth of modern bioengineering, an extraordinary field applying engineering principles to biology and medicine. Since 1943, when Kolff's artificial kidney made its debut in Holland, kidney dialysis has saved the lives of hundreds of thousands of people around the world. Some 40,000 Americans are alive today because of it. The artificial kidney was followed by the heart-lung machine (in which Kolff also had a hand). Soon afterward, bioengineering began to produce a cornucopia of spare parts: cardiac pacemak-

Wearable artificial kidney weighs only eight pounds, is easily carried and could be used almost anywhere.

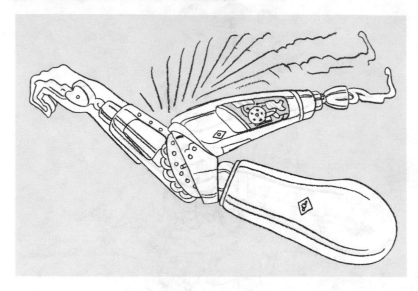

Artificial arm operates more efficiently than previous models.

ers, patches, valves and bypass units, artificial arteries, joints and amazing limbs. It has also produced experimental models of artificial lungs, eyes, ears, livers, pancreases and hearts.

So splendid are these achievements that bioengineering has become the victim of its own success. Rapid progress in space technology, the advent of miniaturized electronic devices and a heady supply of research funds have inspired unrealistic expectations about artificial organs and limbs—as seen in TV shows about a "six-million-dollar man" and a "bionic woman" whose manufactured parts give them superhuman powers.

Yet the pioneers of bioengineering do see their field on the verge of a new flowering. The future they envision includes a whole new family of instruments to monitor body chemistry, computer systems to provide instant medical diagnosis and perhaps even treatment, synthetic materials tailor-made for use inside the body, and new tools for research into the mysteries of such diseases as atherosclerosis, cancer and schizophrenia.

Dr. Kolff has attracted an energetic and talented group of researchers to the University of

Utah, which he joined in 1967. As a result, some of the most exciting work in bioengineering is now taking place in Salt Lake City, where surgeons, mathematicians, physiologists, mechanical engineers, metallurgists, electrical engineers, anesthesiologists, chemists, computer scientists, veterinarians and hematologists form a team in which the solution of one problem helps to deal with another. A variety of these projects are about to pay off.

There is, for example, the Wearable Artificial Kidney, or WAK—a device that could make the lives of thousands of kidney patients more bearable because it would allow many patients to treat themselves comfortably and more cheaply at home, rather than in hospitals or other institutions. At present, people who undergo dialysis must generally lie down and stay connected to a bulky machine for five hours three times a week—a demoralizing and fatiguing experience. However, with the help of a WAK, which packs in a suitcase and weighs only eight pounds (3.63 kilograms), one patient was able to travel to California recently and work at his desk even during the treat-

ments. He was also free to disconnect himself from the tank that contained the blood-cleansing fluid for as much as 15 minutes at a time during the treatment, to open the door or do anything else he liked.

The WAK was designed by Dr. Stephen Jacobscn, an associate professor of mechanical engineering who also runs the university's large Projects and Design Laboratory, where all the parts and supplies for the WAK were made.

Like many of the Utah bioengineers, Dr. Jacobsen is a dynamic man who tackles several different problems at once. Besides working on kidney devices, he has been designing an artificial arm which amputees will be able to move just by thinking about it. In an office lined with medical antiques—such as an 1866 artificial hand made of leather and metal—Jacobsen described the plight of thousands of persons who have lost an arm above the elbow. In many cases these people wear artificial limbs which serve little more than a cosmetic purpose since anything more functional is noisy, heavy, awkward and difficult to operate. So Jacobsen tried something new. Instead of relying on gear trains, screws and pul-

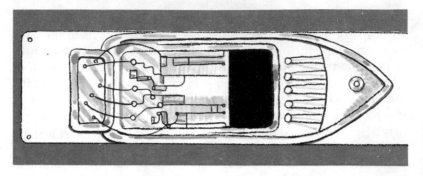

This device (only a millimeter wide), implanted in a patient's arm, would function like a tiny hospital chemistry lab, giving information about the patient's blood.

leys, he designed an artificial muscle made of flexible plastic fibers that works much like the real thing. This, he believes, can provide graceful motion. Then he studied the exact role of 30 separate muscles which are involved in arm motion to identify those which could be used to control an artificial arm. He made a map of the electrical signals from the muscles in the amputee's shoulder and remnant limb, which can be picked up by electrodes in the artificial arm's socket. Finally Jacobsen and his colleagues designed an "anthropomorphic hook," with forefinger and thumb, to serve as an artificial hand. The arm can grasp objects delicately, lift four pounds (1.81 kilograms) actively and withstand loads of up to 50 pounds (22.7 kilograms). For cosmetic reasons, the team added a lifelike plastic glove, complete with finger creases and nails, which can be slipped over the hook to look like a real hand.

An amputee who receives a "Utah arm" will not have to learn complex rules of operation as he or she would with other kinds of full-arm prosthesis. The patient will simply think of moving an elbow or hand, and a microcomputer, which processes signals from the shoulder muscles, will deliver the right amount of energy to motors in the appropriate parts of the arm. So far, the arm has been used only in Jacobsen's lab, but preliminary models will be tried out by amputees under normal conditions, to be followed by models that allow full and graceful motion of the entire arm, the elbow, the wrist and the hand.

Meanwhile, in another part of the university, Dr. Donald J. Lyman, a polymer chemist, is working on a macaroni-sized artificial blood vessel which can flex and pulsate as if it were made of living cells. The material for it was tailormade in Lyman's lab so that it would not clot blood and would be able to form a good junction with natural blood vessels.

This kind of research, he notes, has implications for the control of atherosclerosis, a disease that is the underlying cause of most heart attacks and strokes. Such research may also lead to new ways of diagnosing cancer, for normal cells will stick to certain surfaces and cancer cells will not.

While all these efforts are going on, an ambitious project which was dreamed up by Dr. Kolff 21 years ago is finally nearing fruition. It is an implantable artificial heart, made of polyurethane parts and powered either by compressed air or by electric batteries. Kolff put a crude model of such a heart in a dog in 1957, but it soon became clear that developing an artificial heart for human beings—would strain every aspect of bioengineering. There were problems of design, materials, power, operating procedures and even controversies about the quality of life with such a device. A lesser man would have given up long ago. Instead, in 1970 Kolff recruited an imaginative medical student, Robert Jarvik, and let him loose on the project. Dr. Jarvik, now a seasoned researcher, believes that a battery-powered artificial heart of his own design could be developed for human use. He also feels that this could save the lives of some 50,000 persons a year—people who might otherwise die from heart attacks, heart disease or during open-heart surgery.

Kolff is optimistic not only about the great advances he has witnessed and helped to engineer in the last 40 years but also on the array of medical problems where bioengineering has not even been applied. "If you want to understand the future of bioengineering," he says, "don't talk to doctors; talk to high school students, whose minds have not been ruined."

Number of Words: 1536 ÷ _____ Minutes Reading Time = Rate _____

I. MAIN IDEA

Four of the following sentences state main ideas from the story, while the others state details. Put a ✓ in front of four main ideas.

_____ **1.** When Dr. Willèm Kolff began practicing medicine in the 1930s, his first patient died of kidney failure.

_____ **2.** The success of the first artificial kidney marked the birth of modern bioengineering.

_____ **3.** By the 21st century, a person may be able to order a replacement for almost every ailing part of the body.

_____ **4.** Dr. Kolff joined the University of Utah in 1967.

_____ **5.** There is the wearable artificial kidney—a device that would allow kidney patients to treat themselves at home.

_____ **6.** Dr. Jacobsen studied the exact role of 30 separate muscles that are involved in arm motion.

_____ **7.** It is now believed that a battery-powered artificial heart could be developed in the near future.

10 points for each correct answer   SCORE: _____

II. REFERENCE

Next to each subject listed in Column A, write the letter of the source in Column B that gives information about it.

	A	B
_____ **1.**	Early signs of cancer	**a.** Chemistry textbook
_____ **2.**	Discovery of X-rays	**b.** Medical dictionary
_____ **3.**	Meaning of "athero-sclerosis"	**c.** American Cancer Society
_____ **4.**	Functions of hydrogen	**d.** Encyclopedia

5 points for each correct answer   SCORE: _____

III. OUTLINING

Complete the following outline by writing the correct answer (a, b, c or d) in its proper place.

   a. Attractive as well as functional
   b. Marked birth of modern bioengineering
   c. Artificial heart
   d. Signals from amputee's muscles can be picked up by electrodes in arm's socket

I.   The artificial kidney
   A.   Developed by Dr. William Kolff
   B .   Has saved lives of hundreds of thousands of people
   C.   _____
       1.   Heart-lung machine developed soon afterward
       2.   Cardiac pacemakers and bypass units followed
II. The artificial arm
   A.   Designed by Dr. Stephen Jacobsen
   B .   Wearer can move the arm just by thinking about it
       1.   _____
       2.   Amputee will not have to learn complex rules
   C.   _____
       1.   Lifelike plastic glove looks like real hand
       2.   Can grasp objects delicately
III. _____
   A.   Being researched by Drs. Kolff and Jarvik
   B .   Made of polyurethane parts

10 points for each correct answer   SCORE: _____

PERFECT TOTAL SCORE: 100   TOTAL SCORE: _____

IV. QUESTIONS FOR THOUGHT

Do you think medical science is justified in helping people to live longer when many of the elderly are forced to live in substandard and demoralizing conditions? Why or why not?

Robert Redford Rides the Outlaw Trail

Robert Redford

We have an abiding impression of the outlaw as a low-life renegade, a violent fool who lived off luck and the gun. We view him as one of society's misbegotten, who had to be hunted down like an animal by morally superior men in white hats. But it was not so. In truth, the line between the "good guy" and the "bad guy" in the West was often blurred, and many of the outlaws, in spite of their errant and often violent natures, were men of extraordinary skill and cunning, who by comparison made lawmen look pathetic.

Over the years I have become increasingly intrigued by the many outlaws who demonstrated wit and brains unmatched by any but the most brilliant in legitimate society. I had heard tales of great landmarks of this period, now mostly buried by time and circumstance: old graves, cabins, caves, saloons, whole towns left unattended. I became interested in a part of the country referred to as the Outlaw Trail. This trail runs from Canada to Mexico.

From 1870 to 1910, it was a lawless area where any man with an outlaw past or a price on his head was free to roam nameless—provided he was good with a gun, fast on a horse, cleverer than the next man, could run as fast as he could cheat, trusted no one, had eyes in the back of his head and a fool's sense of adventure.

I wanted to see for myself what remained before it was

too late. And, wherever possible, I wanted to see it the way the outlaws had—by horse and by foot—documenting the adventure with text and photographs. Eight people joined me in the ride. The common denominator was a love of the West or involvement of some sort in its history and progress.

It was mid-October, the transition period between the fading glow of summer and the hueless setting-in of winter, when all is shrouded in muted yellow. A few aspen trees struggled to hold their awesome yellows against winter's color drain.

About one-fourth of the way along the Outlaw Trail is the small town of Kaycee, Wyoming, where the members of our party met. Together we rode into the campsite in Barnum, just east of the famed Hole-in-the-Wall, a spot that derives its name from a niche in the Great Red Wall of Cliffs extending many miles to the south. As everyone settled in for introductions and the filling of cups around the fire, I could see in the distance the famed "hole," where we would be heading in the morning. A V-shaped opening at the top of the Red Wall, it looked barely wide enough to allow passage

of a horse and rider, let alone a wagon.

Our campsite was on the old outlaw ranch, where six log cabins had stood in a semi-compound similar to a fortress. None is left today; all that remains is one cabin foundation hidden in sagebrush.

According to Garvin Taylor, the barrel-chested, gravel-voiced owner of a nearby ranch who would lead our party in, Hole-in-the-Wall is a place that has its own ways, dictated by the outlaws who settled it, and nothing much has changed.

As we saddled up the next morning, Garvin spoke of the Hole-in-the-Wall Valley: "This valley in between these great cliffs is where the outlaws grazed their stolen cattle. At times there were as many as 400 or 500 people encamped here." The valley was ruled by outlaws for 25 or 30 years. Here the outlaws planned future robberies, escaped from recent ones and, by many accounts, had a high old time training horses to do stunts, racing and taking target practice. We got to the top of the cliffs where the hole was. As with so many experiences involving some danger, the rewards were rich. The view was magnificent, and

Redford and traveling party cook dinner around a blazing fire.

suddenly all the history, the geography and the meaning of Hole-in-the-Wall came together. It was at this spot that the Outlaw Trail entered the valley. Its penetration in the wall is so small that two men with Winchester rifles could hold off an entire army. Beyond the opening where we stood there was no access to Hole-in-the-Wall from the east. To the west, south and part of the north extended a sea of grassy plains that provided ample grazing for the outlaws' stolen herds. Here the cattle would idle and be fattened on abundant hay and then rebranded for illegal sale elsewhere.

Talk turned to the threat to the valley. "An irrigation company wants to dam up part of this valley on the Powder River and send water to a power plant a hundred miles away in Gillette," said one of the men. "The water rights are to be purchased by oil companies who have a big interest in the plant. A dam would wipe out our ranch and a lot of others." He sounded sad and bitter.

The way down to Casper, Wyoming, was hideously marred by an almost freakish mutation in the beautiful yawning expanse of space and plain—an oil development.

Our route took us down through the Wind River range and into Atlantic City, Wyoming, an old mining town 7 miles off the main route. A slightly marked dirt road leads into a cup of a valley, where, to our amazement and joy, everything seemed to have been preserved as in an old photograph. A few cabins stood like wooden sentries against stark brown and white slopes.

From Atlantic City, we traveled by car to our next horse-and-saddle station—Brown's Park, Utah. Perhaps no single location in the West, and certainly none on the Outlaw Trail, has had such a varied history as Brown's Park. Located at the border of northeast

Utah and northwest Colorado, just south of Wyoming, Brown's Park is a 40-mile square, half in Utah and half in Colorado.

Brown's Park became a favorite wintering place for cattle herds being driven from Texas to Montana. It is said that the park was the most lawless place in the entire West. The law didn't come to Brown's Park until the turn of the century. Very little was sacred, and shallow graves were common. The only law was that of the fastest gun—some 170 graves are known throughout the park. But even without the standard form of civilized law and order, there was a systematic, if rough, social order. There was a school for children of the park, the grocery store, a blacksmith shop, a saloon and other accoutrements of community living. Conspicuously absent, of course, was a jail.

According to local lore, it was at Cassidy Point in Brown's Park on August 18, 1896, that plans were formulated to organize what Butch Cassidy proposed to call the Train Robbers' Syndicate but which later came to be known as the Wild Bunch. Over 200 outlaws from all the prominent regional gangs were in attendance at

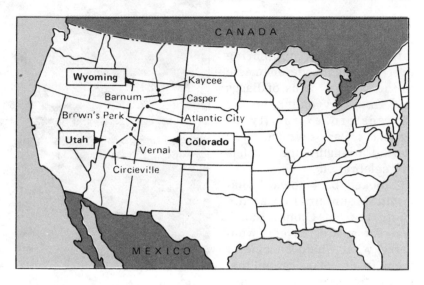

that meeting, including members of the Hole-in-the-Wall Gang.

A conference of sorts was held in a cabin here, and it was agreed that an organization was needed, but there was a dispute between Cassidy and Kid Curry over who was best qualified to lead it. Tense moments passed until someone—probably Butch—came up with the idea of a contest.

It was a simple idea. They would meet again at Brown's Park in one year—on August 18, 1897. During that year two groups—one led by Cassidy, the other by Kid Curry—would pull off various robberies. Whoever was most successful, most spectacular and dar-ing would become the leader.

By the following August, Cassidy, with the aid of Elza Lay, Bob Meeks and Joe Walker, had successfully pulled off several robberies, the most spectacular being the robbery of the Castle Gate payroll of the Pleasant Valley Coal Company on April 21, 1897. During that period Kid Curry together with Flatnose George Curry, the Sundance Kid and several others attempted to hold up the bank at Belle Fourche, South Dakota. They were pursued and captured but escaped from the jail at Deadwood. It was obvious that Cassidy had won.

After the installation of Butch Cassidy as leader of the

Train Robbers' Syndicate at Cassidy Point, the entire outlaw community, numbering over 200 men, rode en masse to the nearby towns of Baggs and Dixon, Wyoming, on the far eastern extremity of Brown's Park, where they started a lengthy and boisterous celebration.

I looked back toward Diamond Mountain to Cassidy Point, the old Crouse Ranch and Parson's cabin and wondered what would become of them. In almost every spot that is not forest or Park Service land, the sprawling hand of the developer can be seen. This area is a natural resource of history threatened by people's encroachment—their need to push ahead, sometimes at any cost.

Wherever I went, I was bothered by what I saw, for I have a genuine love for the people I met along the way. The fiber of these people can only be admired. They show a quality of grit and courage that is ancestral. And in a system where change is inevitable, one can only hope that change can be made without trading off the good qualities of the land and the people, gained through years of pioneering, hardship and enterprise.

We drove down to Vernal, Utah, through more great country of unfolding variety. The next way station on the Outlaw Trail was Robbers' Roost. Here we hooked up with a man named A. C. Ekker and his father, Arthur, who would outfit our ride into more desolate country.

A. C. Ekker is an energetic young man who runs an outfit called Outlaw Trails, Inc. A. C., part of a large pioneer family, is a hardworking and hard-riding ex-rodeo cowboy who suggests, more than anyone I've

come across, the verve, strength, enthusiasm and enterprise attributed to the early settlers and outlaws. In a sinking society of depression and fatalism, of worn leather and tired spirits, he stands out as a leader—forward-looking, hopeful, suggestive of the ability to bring it all together single-handedly. The Outlaw Trails, Inc., venture is largely his doing, and its maintenance and success are his province. Ekker was going to be our guide for the most rugged segment of the trail ride.

Ekker knows this country well and where the few springs are along the way. The area was ideal for the outlaw in this respect—no posse could ever seem to learn where the water holes were, while the outlaws, having memorized the routes through the region and the locations of the springs, would purposely lead the chase parties astray.

"Robbers' Roost was the last and perhaps most unique of the three big way stations along the trail," Ekker explained. "This was desolate country, and it was virtually impossible to follow a lead."

He told us how the outlaws would rustle their cattle into the Roost, which was a 5-mile circular flat that had lookout points on all sides. The Roost is identifiable by two flat-topped buttes on the edge of the flat, facing east and north. It provided the outlaws with caves in which to store their weapons, bunkhouses, saloons and such essentials as disguised hollowed-out trees for the posting of letters and messages. Isolated from settlements by miles of desert and box canyons, it was almost inaccessible except to the few who knew the route. Many lawmen brave or foolish enough to try to penetrate the refuge were lost in the mazes or perished from thirst. Because the outlaws knew where the vital springs were, they could survive.

A. C. talked about how honorable Butch had been—always leaving something for the ranchers, taking care of them in return for their help. And he always kept his word. Cassidy cultivated rancher friendships to great advantage—they were valuable in times of trouble. For their part, the ranchers would deny having seen Cassidy at all. It was a day when a

piece of paper wasn't necessary for an agreement. The rule of word—what if you broke it?

"Well," said A. C., "then someone would show up sooner or later and put a bullet in you to square the deal."

At around six the next morning I awoke to find 5 inches of fresh snow covering my sleeping bag. The sky was gray and flat and cold. It felt cold and looked cold.

Out of some concern and apprehension, we ate a huge breakfast, saddled up and headed out for the Roost flats, where an outlaw stronghold had been and where Butch Cassidy's hideout cave still exists.

It was about 10 miles (16 kilometers) to the Roost and down into the small cut where Butch Cassidy's rock and cave were. The clear day was so cold that frostbite became a real threat. We stopped by Butch's rock and built a midday fire to cook lunch and get warm.

We put our horses in the original corral while we ate. Rocks like red sentinels were behind us, Dirty Devil Canyon was below us and a view of the Henry Mountains was 75 miles in the distance. Everyone was awestruck. We were 15 miles

Nearing the end of their trail, riders warm up around a campfire flanked by looming rocks.

from our campsite, and once again we were made aware of the toughness of the people who had settled here. I looked at us all around the fire, gloved, jacketed, hunched over the warmth, and then at A. C. and his father working with the saddles, collecting wood without gloves, seemingly oblivious of the elements. "You have no choice," said Art Ekker.

Afterward we circled the entire Roost area to see vestiges of the outlaw society. Cassidy's camp had been the center of all activity in the region. Even

people who weren't considered outlaws but were friends of Cassidy's came to the camp to play poker and enter into horse races with the sporty members of the gang. It is said that Butch was the most amiable of all the Western outlaws, and there has been no evidence to disprove this.

It seemed only fitting that we finish our trail ride at the home in which Butch Cassidy grew up and celebrate with a visit to Butch's sister, Lula Betenson, who is in her nineties and lives in the town of Circleville, Utah.

The Outlaw Trail does not end here; it divides into arteries leading east, west and south. But a visit with Lula—my friend since the filming of "Butch Cassidy and the Sundance Kid"—would complete the story for me.

Lula, one of 13 children, was six years old when Butch left home, but she has saved his letters and personal belongings all these years. To this day, she stays in touch with all the surviving relatives of the Wild Bunch by letters and visits. She has outlasted husbands and most of her offspring and now lives with one of her two remaining sons, Mark.

As we pulled in at the white frame house at the end of a dirt road, we were greeted warmly. I was struck by Lula's beauty, even at this age. She is tall and elegant, a proud person who enjoys living. She asked us why we all moved around so much, what the rush was, and said she hoped we were all getting something out of it.

We went out to the original homestead. It was late afternoon and a light autumn breeze was blowing leaves around the land. Lula told me she had lost the sight in one eye and was starting to lose it in the other. She feared that blindness might bring loss of her real spirit. Then she took hold of my arm and looked at me straight on. "I'm fightin' the melancholy," she said. "Don't like good-byes . . . can't stand 'em. Never used to bother me."

She seemed cameo-locket pretty standing there in the late afternoon sun, framed by the cottonwood trees and the old cabin. Such a youthful countenance, with young eyes pleading not to be covered by the cruel mask of old age. Her mind is 30 years or more younger and her desire is as strong as a young girl's.

The house is old. Gray, splintered, sagging wood. The window frames are bleached, and vandalism and target practice have left smashed panes. The rooms are small, like all the rooms in all the buildings of this kind we visited. In the back are the corral fences—gray, shaggy, tilting against the burnt yellow and gray hills beyond.

It's all that's left. Lula and the corrals and the hills. There's no more.

Number of Words: 2805 ÷ _____ Minutes Reading Time = Rate _____

I. SUPPORTING DETAILS

Put a check √ next to three statements that support the idea that the old West is fast disappearing.

_____ **1.** The scheduled dam will wipe out Curt's ranch.

_____ **2.** The way down to Casper, Wyoming was marred by an oil development.

_____ **3.** Hole-in-the-Wall is where outlaws grazed their stolen cattle.

_____ **4.** In almost every spot that is not forest or Park Service land, the hand of the developer can be seen.

10 points for each correct answer   SCORE: _____

II. OUTLINING

Complete the outline below by copying the following names in their proper places below.

    a. the Sundance Kid
    b. Kid Curry
    c. Hole-in-the-Wall
    d. Brown's Park

  I. The Three Big Outlaw Headquarters on the Outlaw Trail
     A. _____
     B. _____
     C. Robber's Roost
 II. Outlaws on the Outlaw Trail
     A. Butch Cassidy
     B. _____
     C. _____

5 points for each correct answer   SCORE: _____

III. FACT/OPINION

Put an F next to the statments of fact and O next to the sentences that express an opinion.

_____ **1.** The line between the "good guy" and the "bad guy" in the West was often blurred.

_____ **2.** Brown's Park is 40 miles square.

_____ **3.** The Outlaw Trail runs from Canada to Mexico.

_____ **4.** "Robbers' Roost" was the last and perhaps most unique of the three big way stations along the trail.

5 points for each correct answer   SCORE: _____

IV. LANGUAGE USAGE

Check two sentences which use figures of speech.

_____ **1.** Rocks like red sentinels were behind us.

_____ **2.** Everything in Atlantic City seemed to have been preserved as in an old photograph.

_____ **3.** The view was marred by an almost freakish mutation.

_____ **4.** A few cabins stood like wooden sentries against the stark brown and white slopes.

15 points for each correct answer   SCORE: _____

PERFECT TOTAL SCORE: 100   TOTAL SCORE: _____

V. QUESTION FOR THOUGHT

Do you agree with the author that from many experiences involving danger the results are rich rewards? Explain.

THE GRIFFIN AND THE MINOR CANON

Frank Stockton

Over the great door of an old church in a quiet town there was carved in stone the figure of a large griffin. The old-time sculptor had done his work with great care, but the image he had made was not a pleasant one to look at. It had a large head with an enormous open mouth and savage teeth; from its back arose great wings armed with sharp hooks and prongs; it had stout legs in front, with projecting claws, but no legs behind—the body running out into a long and powerful tail, finished off at the end with a barbed point.

This tail was coiled up under it, the end sticking up just behind the wings.

A distance from the town, in the midst of dreadful wilds scarcely known to man, there dwelt the Griffin whose image had been put up over the church door. In some way or other, the old-time sculptor had seen him and afterward, to the best of his memory, had copied his figure in stone.

The Griffin had never known this, until, hundreds of years afterward, he heard in some manner which it is not now easy to find out, that there was a likeness of him on the old church in the distant town.

When he heard of this stone image of himself, he became very anxious to know what he looked like, and at last he determined to go to the old church and see for himself what manner of being he was.

The news of his coming spread quickly over the town, and the people, frightened nearly out of their wits by the arrival of so strange a visitor, fled into their houses and shut themselves up. The Griffin called loudly for someone to come to him but the more he called, the more afraid the people were to show themselves. At length he saw two laborers hurrying to their homes through the fields, and in a terrible voice he commanded them to stop. Not daring to disobey, the men stood, trembling.

"What is the matter with you all?" cried the Griffin. "Is there not a man in your town who is brave enough to speak to me?"

"I think," said one of the laborers, his voice shaking so that his words could hardly be understood, "that—perhaps—the Minor Canon—would come."

"Go call him, then!" said the Griffin, "I want to see him."

The Minor Canon, who was an assistant in the old church, had just finished the afternoon services and was coming out of a side door with three aged women who had formed the weekday congregation. He was a young man of a kind disposition and very anxious to do good for the people of the town. Whenever the people wanted something difficult done for them, they always went to the Minor Canon. Thus it was that the laborer thought of the young priest when he found that someone must come and speak to the Griffin.

The Minor Canon had not heard of the strange event, and when he was informed of it and was told that the Griffin had asked to see him, he was

greatly amazed and frightened.

"Me!" he exclaimed. "He has never heard of me! What should he want with me?"

"Oh! you must go instantly!" cried the two men. "He is very angry now because he has been kept waiting so long. And nobody knows what may happen if you don't hurry to him."

The poor Minor Canon would rather have had his hand cut off than go out to meet an angry Griffin. But he felt that it was his duty to go, for it would be a woeful thing if injury should come to the people of the town because he was not brave enough to obey the summons of the Griffin. So,

pale and frightened, he started off.

"Well," said the Griffin, as soon as the young man came near, "I am glad to see that there is someone who has the courage to come to me."

The Minor Canon did not feel very brave, but he bowed his head.

"Is this the town," said the Griffin, "where there is a church with a likeness of myself over one of the doors?"

The Minor Canon looked at the frightful creature before him and saw that it was, without doubt, exactly like the stone image on the church. "Yes," he said, "you are right."

"Well, then," said the Griffin, "will you take me to it? I wish very much to see it."

The Minor Canon instantly thought that if the Griffin entered the town without the people's knowing what he came for, some of them would probably be frightened to death, and so he sought to gain time to prepare their minds.

"It is growing dark, now," he said, very much afraid as he spoke that his words might enrage the Griffin, "and objects on the front of the church cannot be seen clearly. It will be better to wait until morning, if you wish to get a good view of the stone image of yourself."

The Minor Canon was glad enough to take his leave, and hurried into the town. In front of the church he found a great many people assembled to hear his report of his interview with the Griffin. When they found that he had not come to spread ruin but simply to see his stony likeness on the church, they showed neither relief nor gratitude but began to upbraid the Minor Canon for consenting to conduct the creature into the town.

"What could I do?" cried the young man. "If I should not bring him he would come himself, and, perhaps, end by setting fire to the town with his red-hot tail."

Still the people were not satisfied, and a great many plans were proposed to prevent the Griffin from coming into the town. Some elderly persons urged that the young men should go out and kill him, but the young men scoffed at such a ridiculous idea.

Bickering continued well into the night. By early morning the people, not having agreed on a plan, began dispersing for their homes. When everyone had gone, the Minor Canon hurried away to the field where he had left the Griffin.

The monster had just awakened and said that he was ready to go into the town. The Minor Canon, therefore, walked back, the Griffin flying slowly through the air, at a short distance above the head of his guide. Not a person was to be seen in the streets, and they went quickly to the front of the church, where the Minor Canon pointed out the stone griffin.

The real Griffin settled down in the little square before the church and gazed earnestly at his sculptured likeness. For a long time he looked at it. After a while he said to the Minor Canon, who had been standing

by all this time, "It is, it must be, an excellent likeness! That breadth between the eyes, that expansive forehead, those massive jaws! I feel that it must resemble me. If there is any fault to find with it, it is that the neck seems a little stiff. But that is nothing. It is an admirable likeness—admirable!"

The Griffin sat looking at his image all that morning and all that afternoon. The Minor Canon had been afraid to go away and leave him. But by evening the poor young man was very tired and felt that he must eat and sleep. He frankly said this to the Griffin and asked him if he would not like something to eat. He said this because he felt obliged in politeness to do so. But as soon as he had spoken the words, he was seized with dread lest the monster should demand half a dozen babies or some other tempting repast of that kind.

"Oh, no," said the Griffin; "I never eat between the equinoxes. At the vernal and at the autumnal equinox I take a good meal, and that lasts me for half a year. I am extremely regular in my habits and do not think it healthful to eat at odd times. But if you need food, go and get it, and I will return to

the soft grass where I slept last night and take another nap."

The next day the Griffin came again to the little square before the church and remained there until evening. And when the people came to the Minor Canon's house and anxiously asked him how long the Griffin was going to stay, he answered, "I do not know, but I think he will soon be satisfied with regarding his stone likeness, and then he will go away."

But the Griffin did not go away. Morning after morning he came to the church, but after a time he did not stay there all day. He seemed to have taken a great fancy to the Minor Canon and followed him about as he worked.

When it was found that the Griffin showed no sign of going away, all the people who were able to do so left the town leav-

ing behind only the Minor Canon and the poor.

Day by day the Griffin became more and more attached to the Minor Canon. He kept near him a great part of the time and often spent the night in front of the little house where the young clergyman lived alone. This strange companionship was often burdensome to the Minor Canon, but, on the other hand, he could not deny that he derived a great deal of benefit and instruction from it. The Griffin had lived for hundreds of years and had seen much, and he told the Minor Canon many wonderful things.

Thus the summer went on and drew toward its close. And now the people of the town began to be very much troubled again.

"It will not be long," they said, "before the autumnal

equinox is here, and then that monster will want to eat. He will be dreadfully hungry for he has taken so much exercise since his last repast. He will devour our children. Without doubt, he will eat them all. What is to be done?"

To this dilemma no one could proffer an answer, but it was unanimous that the Griffin must not be allowed to remain until the approaching equinox. After talking over the situation a great deal, a crowd of the people went to the Minor Canon at a time when the Griffin was not with him.

"It is all your fault that the monster is among us," they said. "You brought him here, and you ought to see that he goes away. It is only on your account that he stays here at all; for, although he visits his image every day, he is with you the greater part of the time. If you were not here, he would not stay. It is your duty to go away, away to the dreadful wilds where the Griffin lives; and then he will follow you and stay there."

They did not say whether or not they expected the Minor Canon to stay there also, and he did not ask them anything about it. He bowed his head and went into his house to think. The more he thought, the more clear it became in his mind that it was his duty to go away and thus free the town from the presence of the Griffin.

That evening he packed a leather bag with bread and meat, and early the next morning he set out on his journey to the dreadful wilds.

When the Griffin found that the Minor Canon had left the town he seemed sorry, but he showed no desire to go and

look for him. After a few days had passed he became much annoyed and asked some of the people where the Minor Canon had gone. Although the citizens had been so anxious that the young clergyman should go to the dreadful wilds, thinking that the Griffin would immediately follow him, they were afraid to mention the Minor Canon's destination. The monster seemed angry enough already, and if he should suspect their trick he would, doubtless, become very much enraged. So everyone said he did not know, and the Griffin wandered about disconsolate.

The summer had now passed, and the autumnal equinox was rapidly approaching. The citizens were in a state of great alarm and anxiety. The Griffin showed no signs of going away but seemed to have settled himself permanently among them. In a short time the day for his semiannual meal would arrive, and then what would happen? The monster would certainly be very hungry and would devour all their children.

Now they greatly regretted and lamented that they had sent away the Minor Canon. He was the only one on whom they could have depended in this trouble, for he could talk freely with the Griffin and so find out what could be done. A meeting of the citizens was called, and two old men were appointed to talk to the Griffin. They were instructed to offer to prepare a splendid dinner for him on equinox day—one that would entirely satisfy his hunger.

The old men went to the Griffin, but their propositions were not received with favor.

"From what I have seen of the people of this town," said the monster, "I do not think I could relish anything that was prepared by them. They appear to be all cowards and, therefore, mean and selfish. As for eating one of them, old or young, I could not think of it for a moment. In fact, there was only one creature in the whole place for whom I could have had any appetite, and that is the Minor Canon, who has gone away. He was brave and good and honest, and I think I should have relished him."

"Ah!" said one of the old men very politely, "in that case I wish we had not sent him to the dreadful wilds!"

"What!" cried the Griffin. "What do you mean? Explain instantly what you are talking about!"

The old man, terribly frightened at what he had said, was obliged to tell how the Minor Canon had been sent away by the people, in the hope that the Griffin might be induced to follow him.

When the monster heard this he became furiously angry. He dashed away from the old men, and, spreading his wings, flew backward and forward over the town. He was so much excited that his tail became red-hot and glowed like a meteor against the evening sky. At last he settled down in the little field where he usually rested and thrust his fiery tail into the brook. The steam arose like a cloud, and the water of the stream ran hot through the town. The citizens were greatly frightened and bitterly blamed the old man for telling about the Minor Canon.

"It is plain," they said, "that the Griffin intended at last to go and look for him, and we should have been saved. Now who can tell what misery you have brought upon us."

The Griffin did not remain long in the little field. As soon as his tail was cool he flew to the town hall and rang the bell. The citizens knew that they were expected to come there. Although they were afraid to go, they were still more afraid to stay away. They crowded into the hall. The Griffin was on the platform at one end, flapping his wings and walking up and down, and the end of his tail was still so warm that it slightly scorched the boards as he dragged it after him.

When everybody who was able to come was there, the Griffin stood still and addressed the meeting.

"I have had a very low opinion of you," he said, "ever since I discovered what cowards you are, but I had no idea that you were so ungrateful, selfish and cruel as I now find you to be. Here was your Minor Canon, who labored day and night for your good and thought of nothing else but how he might benefit you and make you happy. And as soon as you imagine yourselves threatened with a danger—for well I know you are dreadfully afraid of me— you sent him off, caring not whether he returns or perishes, hoping thereby to save yourselves. Now, I had conceived a great liking for that young man and had intended, in a day or two, to go and look him up. But I have changed my mind about him. I shall go and find him, but I shall send him back here to live among you, and I intend that he shall enjoy the reward

of his labor and his sacrifices.

If, when your Minor Canon comes back to you, you do not bow yourselves before him, put him in the highest place among you and serve and honor him all his life, beware of my terrible vengeance! There were only two good things in this town: the Minor Canon and the stone image of myself over your church door. One of these you have sent away, and the other I shall carry away myself."

The next morning the Griffin came to the church, and, tearing the stone image of himself from its fastenings over the monumental door, he grasped it with his powerful forelegs and swooped up into the air. Then, after hovering over the town for a moment, he gave his tail an angry shake and took up his flight to the dreadful wilds. When he reached this desolate region, he set the stone griffin upon a ledge of a rock that rose in front of the dismal cave he called his home. There the image occupied a position somewhat similar to the one it had had over the church door. The Griffin, panting with the exertion of carrying such an enormous load to so great a distance, lay down upon the ground and regarded it with much satisfaction. When he felt somewhat rested, he went to look for the Minor Canon.

He found the young man, weak and half starved, lying under the shadow of a rock. After picking him up and carrying him to his cave, the Griffin flew away to a distant marsh, where he procured some roots and herbs that he well knew were strengthening and beneficial to man, though he had never tasted them himself. After eating these, the Minor Canon was greatly revived and sat up and listened while the Griffin told him what had happened in the town.

"Do you know," said the

monster, when he had finished, "that I have had, and still have, a great liking for you?"

"I am very glad to hear it," said the Minor Canon with his usual politeness.

"I am not at all sure that you would be," said the Griffin, "if you thoroughly understood the state of the case. But we will not consider that now. If some things were different, other things would be otherwise. I have been so enraged by discovering the manner in which you have been treated that I have determined that you shall at last enjoy the rewards and honors to which you are entitled. Lie down and have a good sleep, and then I will take you back to the town."

As he heard these words, a look of consternation came over the young man's face.

"You need not give yourself any anxiety," said the Griffin, "about my return to the town. I shall not reside there any longer. Now that I have that admirable likeness of myself in front of my cave, where I can sit at my leisure and gaze upon its noble features and magnificent proportions, I have no wish to see that abode of cowardly and selfish people."

The Minor Canon, relieved of his anxiety, lay back and dropped into a doze. When he was sound asleep, the Griffin took him up and carried him back to the town. He arrived just before daybreak. After setting the young man gently on the grass in the little field where he himself used to rest, the monster, without having been seen by any of the people, flew back to his home.

When the Minor Canon made his appearance in the morning among the citizens, the enthusiasm and cordiality with which he was received were truly wonderful. He was taken to a house that had been occupied by one of the banished high officers of the place, and everyone was anxious to do all that could be done for his health and comfort. The people crowded into the church when he held services. The three old women who used to be his weekday congregation could not get to the best seats, which they had always been in the habit of taking. And the parents of the bad children determined to reform them at home, in order that he might be spared the trouble of keeping up his former school. The Minor Canon was appointed to the highest office of the old church, and before he died he became a bishop.

During the first years after his return from the dreadful wilds, the people of the town looked up to him as a man to whom they were bound to do honor and reverence. But they often, also, looked up to the sky to see if there were any signs of the Griffin coming back. However, in the course of time, they learned to honor and revere their former Minor Canon without the fear of being punished if they did not do so.

But they need never have been afraid of the Griffin. The autumnal equinox day came around, and the monster ate nothing. If he could not have the Minor Canon, he did not care for anything. So, lying down, with his eyes fixed upon the great stone griffin, he gradually declined and died. It was a good thing for some of the people of the town that they did not know this.

If you should ever visit the old town, you would still see the little griffins on the sides of the church. But the great stone griffin that was over the door is gone.

Number of Words: 3753 ÷ _____ Minutes Reading Time = Rate _____

I. CRITICAL THINKING

Circle the letter (a, b or c) that correctly completes each of the following sentences.

1. If the townspeople had not been cowardly and cruel
   a. the Griffin would not have liked them.
   b. the Griffin would probably have eaten the Minor Canon.
   c. the Griffin would have taken care of them.

2. The Griffin
   a. was wise and outspoken.
   b. was a selfish creature.
   c. used the Minor Canon.

3. The people of the town
   a. were liberal in their views.
   b. were fearful of the Griffin.
   c. had legitimate reasons for their behavior.

10 points for each correct answer   SCORE: _____

II. INFERENCES

Put a check ✓ next to three ideas that can be inferred from the story.

_____ 1. The townspeople were more cruel and barbaric than the Griffin.

_____ 2. The townspeople began to like the Griffin.

_____ 3. The Griffin was a proud creature.

_____ 4. The Minor Canon was a foolish and ridiculous man.

_____ 5. The Minor Canon was an unselfish person.

_____ 6. The Griffin was a timid man.

10 points for each correct answer   SCORE: _____

III. CAUSE/EFFECT

Each set of sentences contains a cause and an effect. Put a C next to the cause and an E next to the effect in each set.

_____ 1. The Griffin remained in town with the Minor Canon.

_____   The people sent the Minor Canon out into the wilds.

_____ 2. The Griffin went into town to view his stone image.

_____   The Griffin didn't know what he looked like.

_____ 3. The Minor Canon was liked by the Griffin.

_____   The Griffin died from lack of a meal.

10 points for each correct answer   SCORE: _____

IV. AUTHOR'S PURPOSE

Put a check ✓ next to the sentence that tells a purpose the author had in writing this story:

_____ 1. to show that different-looking things are to be feared

_____ 2. to show that it does not pay to have good intentions

_____ 3. to show that people are often stimulated to do something only when they fear a terrible consequence

10 points for correct answer   SCORE: _____

PERFECT TOTAL SCORE: 100   TOTAL SCORE: _____

V. QUESTIONS FOR THOUGHT

Do you think it is wise to prejudge people or situations during the course of life? Are things always as they appear?